Artisan Bristol

SOPHIE REES

Artisan Bristol

SOPHIE REES

The
History
Press

Front cover image courtesy of Babs Behan.

First published 2019

97 St George's Place
Cheltenham
Gloucestershire
GL50 3QB
www.thehistorypress.co.uk

British Library Cataloguing in Publication Data.
A catalogue record for this book is available from the British Library.

ISBN 978 0 7509 8934 3

Design by Jemma Cox
Printed in China

Contents

Introduction   7

Jane Kenney   Angie Parker
Jewellery Designer   10   *Weaver*   44

Katie Wallis   Libby Ballard
Surface Designer   15   *Ceramicist*   50

Milly Melbourne   Liz Vidal
Fashion Designer   22   *Ceramicist*   57

Sophie Woodrow   Anna Gravelle
Ceramicist   29   *Textile Artist*   63

Stephanie Tudor   Amber Hards
Visual Artist   37   *Knitwear Designer*   72

Catriona R. MacKenzie
Glassblower   78

Charlotte Duckworth
Silversmith   85

Jacky Puzey
Digital Embroiderer   91

Oliver Cross and Lucy Lloyd
Footwear Designers   98

Rosalyn Faith
Jewellery Designer   104

Rachel Foxwell
Ceramicist   110

Ami Pepper
Jewellery Designer   116

Eily O'Connell
Jewellery Designer   121

Jennifer Orme
Ceramicist   125

Kate Bond
Surface Designer   132

Sarah Wilton
Ceramicist   137

Jessica Thorn
Ceramicist   143

Juliet Bailey and Franki Brewer
Textile Designers   150

Phoebe Smith
Ceramicist   157

Babs Behan
Botanical Artist   163

About the Author   169
Acknowledgements   171
Image Credits   172
References   174

Introduction

Ceramicists, shoemakers, glassblowers, jewellers, weavers, leatherworkers; Bristol is the hub of South West England and a city that thrives on creativity. Often hailed as the UK's best place to live, Bristol is a dynamic city and is currently seeing a surge of designer/makers choosing to live and work here. As in my own case, many people working within the creative industries are choosing to leave their hectic and expensive lifestyle in London for a more laid-back pace without compromising on the number of artistic and cultural opportunities on their doorstep.

This decision is obviously paying off for many people, a 2016 study by the University of the West of England (UWE), the University of Bristol and Bath Spa University found that designers living and working within the Bristol and Bath region have higher levels of productivity than the rest of England and Wales. The report, 'Bristol and Bath by Design', shows that design-led companies based in the region have a 3–5 per cent higher turnover of income than design companies elsewhere in the country.

Although there are obviously fewer options than in London or other capital cities, there are plenty of excellent outlets for art and design, with cinemas, restaurants and music venues normally a short walk away. On top of that, Bristol is surrounded by beautiful countryside, stunning coastlines and is just over an hour from the Brecon Beacons and Dartmoor National Park. From a work perspective, there are very active creative and entrepreneurial communities throughout Bristol, and with great rail, bus and air links you can get to many major UK and European cities pretty quickly.

Bristol has a well documented history of supporting crafts. In medieval Bristol wool was woven and dyed then exported alongside leather goods. In the later seventeenth century a glass industry prospered in Bristol; due to its strategic location and shipbuilding industry, trade thrived and it became the most important place for the glassmaking industry in Europe at the time. It also had easy access to other raw materials used in glassmaking, such as sand from the Redcliffe Caves, kelp from Bridgwater, and clay from further north along the Severn.

By the late eighteenth century there were some twenty glassmaking firms in Bristol. Most made crownglass (for windows) or bottles, but a good proportion made a beautiful range of flint glass tableware that was to become the city's legacy.

Bristol Museum has one of the largest collections of English delftware, representing a major industry in and around the city from the 1640s until 1785. Delftware gave way to ordinary earthenwares, in particular those made by the firm Pountney, which survived in the city until 1969. There were two porcelain factories; the factory owned by Benjamin Lund made imitation or 'soft-paste' porcelains until William Cookworthy created 'Bristol Ware', an English true or 'hard-paste' porcelain similar to that of the Chinese and Germans. He opened his Bristol-based factory in 1770, starting a trend for Bristol-based potteries.

Bristol has always attracted craftspeople, inventors and entrepreneurs. *Artisan Bristol* is the culmination of interviews and studio visits made over several months with twenty-five designer/makers and reveals their personal relationship with Bristol and how the city influences their day-to-day practice. Each profile contains a selection of photos captured during the studio visits, offering an intimate portrait of these makers at work.

Sophie Rees, 2019

Jane Kenney

JEWELLERY DESIGNER

Hailing from Nottinghamshire, Jane moved to Bristol fifteen years ago after completing her degree at Loughborough University with a BA Hons in Jewellery and Silversmithing. Taking up a job with renowned Bristol jeweller Diana Porter at her shop on Park Street, Jane is grateful to Diana for the opportunity and for introducing her to the city she now calls home. 'I love Bristol! When I moved here fifteen years ago it quite quickly felt like home, I stayed here for a couple of years and then moved away but found that I really missed Bristol.'

In 2005, Jane took the leap and set up her own label, based in Bristol and sourcing materials from Birmingham Jewellery Quarter. Working predominantly in silver, Jane creates versatile, wearable pieces for everyday adornment alongside one-off commissions such as engagement rings in various precious metals. Each piece is hammered by hand to create unusual textures and shapes, which also leaves a mark of individuality and a sense of the handmade. 'I started adding texture to my work when I found a hammer in my Dad's workshop that belonged to my Grandpa.'

A self-confessed night owl, Jane likes to work from her home studio, which is a self-build at the bottom of her garden. This fits around her day spent completing admin tasks whilst caring for her son, Sullivan, and taking her dog, Peggy, for strolls along Bristol harbourside, a never-ending source of inspiration.

In the evening, Jane makes a big cup of tea before heading down the garden to start work, perhaps with a podcast on in the background (the 'Do Lectures' and 'How To Curate Your Life' are favourites). Building and making with her hands developed from a love of art and design at school: sculpture, 3D design and then jewellery design. Her work doesn't focus on a particular theme but is developed through experimentation with process and materials. Future collections will build on this and also include precious metals and stones.

Jane sells most of her work through her website and a few select stockists in the UK. Taking part in craft fairs, exhibitions and trade shows has always been an enjoyable way to connect with her clients and meet with galleries: however, with recent motherhood that has been put on a backburner as the preparation can be all consuming.

Like many creative people, it is difficult to balance time spent creating against everything that comes with running a business – PR and social media alone can take up a whole day if you let it, so having a weekly 'action plan' helps Jane stay focused and prioritise her workload. Her studio is by far the most organised I have seen, with calendars, lists and schedules all in place to make the week run smoothly.

Alongside her own collection, Jane launched project 'Strange' with her husband, Gavin Strange (designer, illustrator and author at The Do Book Co.), a few years ago. It is an online shop selling their collaborative work in jewellery design, and homeware, furniture and stationery by other designers based in the UK. Jane and Gavin hand-pick items from a selection of their favourite independent makers, offering a wide range of styles that reflect their combined tastes.

Having a creative support network is so important, especially when working from home, as it can often be isolating. Jane is lucky to have found a large group of jewellers in Bristol who quickly became friends and offer ongoing support and advice. Jane has found that feeling part of a community is vital, especially in the very first years after leaving university when you are used to having a community around you. 'I also have many friends who are self-employed creatives, ranging from illustrators, potters and graphic designers; being able to discuss and share experiences is reassuring.'

Jane also looks to her contemporaries for inspiration: Ruth Tomlinson, Polly Wales, Mirri Damer, Alison Macleod and Ami Pepper (featured in this book) are among some of her favourite makers for their use of precious stones with a strong individual aesthetic.

www.janekenney.co.uk

Katie Wallis

SURFACE DESIGNER

Katie is a multidisciplinary surface designer, creating digitally designed and printed patterns. Her distinctive colour pallet and playful use of scale and shape has been described as 'metamorphic modernism'. The motifs are inspired by animals she admires, specifically bees, butterflies, peacocks and a mammal she initially found repellant and rather creepy – the bat. Patterns often reference symmetry, geometry and colour, covering subjects like the colour of pollens, the bee dance, camouflage and echolocation. Most of her fabrics are digitally printed, her mirrors are laser cut and either screen printed or painted with specialist effects.

Katie makes her fabrics into hand-rolled lampshades, cushions, scarves and other smaller gift products, and is currently expanding the range into wallpaper, curtains and decorative panels. Once she has completed her designs, they are digitally printed onto fabric at the Glasgow School of Art. Katie dyes her organically sourced backing fabrics in small batches in her washing machine and completes the laser cutting locally in Bristol. The screen printing and painting of her decorative mirror frames is done in her home studio. 'My patterns have been pretty much solely about pollinators: bees, bats and butterflies, with the exception of the occasional peacock, just because I love them. Symmetry and relevant colour play major parts in their construction.'

Inspiration comes in many forms; the work of architect William Burgess and the Glasgow designers Timourous Beasties are particularly high on the list. Holidays abroad to Italy, France and Portugal, flora and fauna, and decorative buildings are a great source of creative ideas. Katie's favourite haunt in London is the V&A, whilst closer to home she enjoys wandering through the botanical gardens in Clifton and the butterfly tent at Bristol Zoo. The flowers and plants in her garden and allotment provide a very closely observed and personal inspiration.

Katie grew up in a creative household in South Wales where she had the freedom to explore her artistic tendencies, painting her first mural on the bedroom wall at age 12. Before heading to university to study illustration, she spent time travelling in India and Sri Lanka, which had a profound effect on her and resulted in an everlasting sensitivity to colour and pattern. After several years in London working as a mural artist, Katie, her printmaker husband and young family moved to Bristol in 2003 to be nearer her mum and sister. Bristol appealed to Katie because of its smaller size and demographic, and its proximity to Wales and the countryside, which she wanted for her children. 'Bristol has all I need: community, culture, ease of access to countryside, and I love its green conscience.'

In 2012, Katie completed an MA in Multidisciplinary Printmaking at the University of the West of England (UWE) and in 2015 she was chosen to take part in the Crafts Council Hothouse scheme. Hothouse has provided a strong network of friends and colleagues in Bristol that all stay in touch and organise regular meetups and events. She is also a part of a small group of multidisciplinary printmakers collectively called IN-sight, who met whilst studying at UWE. They have exhibited together every couple of years and at the time of writing are planning to exhibit at The Museum in the Park in Stroud, where they have been given access to the museum's stores. Each is creating new pieces of work inspired by what they have found, in a diverse variety of printmaking techniques.

Katie has also been involved in the Bristol-born and much loved 'Grand Appeal' project, the 'Shaun in the City' sculpture trail, and 2018's 'Gromit Unleashed 2' trail, which saw over sixty sculptures dotted around the city. They were a mixture of Aardman characters (Wallace, Gromit, Shaun the Sheep and Feathers McGraw) adapted and painted by local artists to raise money for Bristol Royal Hospital for Children. The project has been an ongoing opportunity for Katie to use both graphic and scenic painting skills.

Katie's studio is a big double room in her house in St Andrews, but she spends quite a lot of time in the living room on the computer too, with a view of the garden and her leafy conservatory, which has one of her original stencil designs painted on the wall. Katie's home is a haven of colour, pattern, illustration and adornment; her collection of green glass paperweights is something to behold!

This arrangement works for her because she can be there when the children get home from school, it's economical and she enjoys having her own space without the compromise that sometimes comes in shared workspaces. Katie separates her time between home and working in her shared gallery/shop, Fig, on Gloucester Road. It's a small shop run by five Bristol-based designer/makers, where you can browse and buy handmade jewellery, embroidery, glass, homewares, art and textiles.

Creative endeavours are an ever-evolving mix; Katie likes to dabble in ceramics, weave, embroidery and stained glass. Her next exploration may be with upholstery, alongside an array of hobbies that include pilates, reading, walks in the countryside and gardening. She is currently developing designs for wallpaper and designing fabric for a collaborative upholstery project. Her dream is to collaborate with interior designers on bespoke projects and design themed rooms for a boutique hotel.

www.katiewallisprint.com

Milly Melbourne

FASHION DESIGNER

Milly Melbourne creates handcrafted objects for everyday play through her brand, oB wear. Reflecting on the relationships we have with the objects in our lives, she seeks to create considered adaptable garments that shape with us over the years, changing their sculptures from person to person and from day to day, inviting playful and curious reflections in the ritual between being naked and fully clothed.

Growing up in small Nottinghamshire village with family living close by, she has a sense of rootedness and a fondness for nostalgia. Milly attributes her interest in textiles to her grandmother, who would make clothes for all the family and taught Milly to sew at a young age. Having the freedom to explore her creative side as a child pushed Milly in the direction of fashion and textiles, spending her teenage years running up her own clothing.

'I was fascinated with buying "old things" from car boots, charity shops and antique shops, filling my room floor to ceiling with these used objects from the past. I would cut things up and start fashioning my own clothes together – I made some pretty odd-looking things to say the least!'

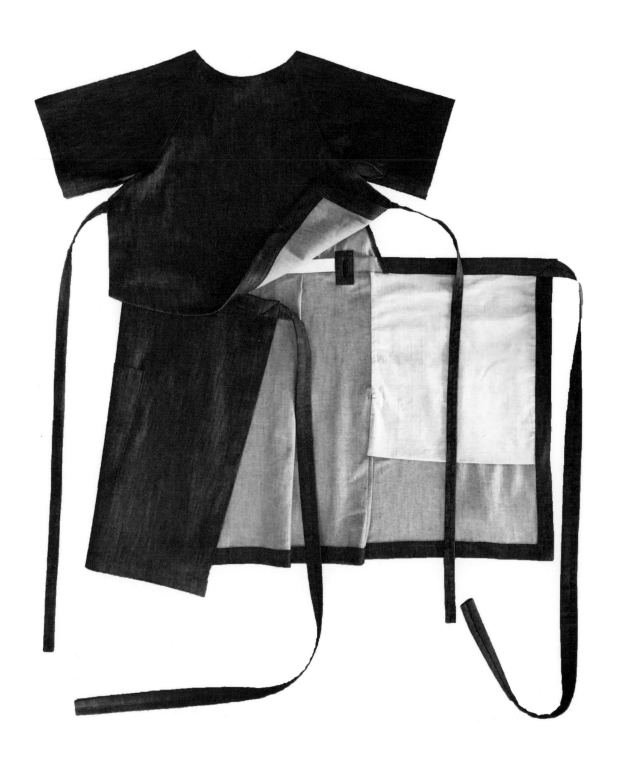

Milly undertook a BTEC in Fashion and Clothing at Nottingham College, which gave her a good footing for a degree in Fashion Design at Falmouth University, which in turn proved to be the perfect fit for her. The course veered away from competitive seasonal fashion trends and instead focused on the craft of making and designing 'real clothes' that would become positive, engaging and practical assets in everyday life.

Graduating in 2014, Milly moved to Bristol in 2017 after completing a residency in Cornwall, where she founded her label oB. Although beautiful and inspiring, the reality of making a living and paying the bills on the Cornish coast didn't add up, so Milly headed for Bristol to pursue its creative reputation and sense of community spirit.

Since then, oB has become more established and Milly has made some great connections through her studio Estate of the Arts in Bedminster (an industrial unit that was an old trailer yard until very recently) and through Bristol's own collective of emerging local textile designers and craftspeople at the Bristol Textile Quarter and The Ottowin Shop.

The studios have now been converted into a creative hub, where Milly works alongside carpenters, sculptors, animators, painters, printers and an array of other designers who inspire her work.

Being part of a growing community of artists has been a great way of transitioning to a new city, offering an instant network of friends with shared interests, and it has opened up new dialogues into creative practices Milly had little knowledge of previously. Bristol echoes much of the creative and community spirit she found whilst living in Cornwall, its entrepreneurial makers, artists, enthusiasts and business owners working within a meaningful practice that holds true to themselves and not letting money be the main driving force.

Milly shares a converted home on wheels with her partner, so depending on where they have parked the night before it's usually a short cycle ride across the city to reach their studio. This sense of freedom is important to Milly, being able to take off and explore a new landscape without the distractions of modern living. Feeling most at home in the countryside, she likes to recharge with just her thoughts and the flora and fauna for company.

Milly likes to pop into the komono shop on Perry Road for inspiration; analysing how the kimonos are cut, sewn and worn. Looking on the inside of the garment to view the hand stitching in detail, she approaches everything with an anthropological mindset, enjoying the journey and purpose of a garment being made as much as the final piece. Her dream commission would be to travel the world discovering the ways humans wear cloth around their bodies, researching the dressing rituals and narratives told through clothing all around the globe and throughout the many different cultures and societies.'Hearing the stories which have clung to a garment that someone loves and understanding how personal value for an object transcends it's material form really moves me and runs core into what I'm trying to make.'

Milly is particularly interested in the act of dressing the body, the performance and interaction we have with cloth day to day. We each see the same object but all interact differently with it; this playfulness forms the basis for the constant evolution in Milly's creations: viewing clothes as wearable sculptures, watching how they transition from something being worn or flopped on a chair to being rolled up in a drawer.

Milly handpicks a variety of ethically sourced materials which offer something other than their textile characteristics, be it organic, fair trade, locally made, naturally dyed, supporting a small family industry or reclaimed. Being transparent is an important element of the brand and Milly spends time hunting down the right fabrics from ethically conscious suppliers and continuing to refine her choices. Recent fabrics used in oB's collection are Lithuanian linen, Belgian linen, Romanian hemp, Indian Khadi cotton, Japanese weaves, organic European cottons, British woven canvases and British wools.

Taking a space at In Bristol Studio has kick-started a stream of collaborative projects and opportunities to develop oB wear. Milly is currently working on a number of projects, including being stocked in Ottowin's very own ethical and independent shop near St Nick's Market in central Bristol. 'Collaborating is really fun and it's my way of growing the brand and sharing my process.'

As a result a few other collaborations have formed; oB and 'Tamay & Me' are going to release a pair of zero waste trousers from the handwoven indigo-dyed fabric that Tamay sources in her hometown in Vietnam. Milly will also be releasing a knitwear collection in collaboration with Bristol knitters and spinners, using locally sourced wool from the South West. Additionally, she will be working with a local carpenter to create objects used for hanging the garments. Watch this space.

www.ob-wear.com

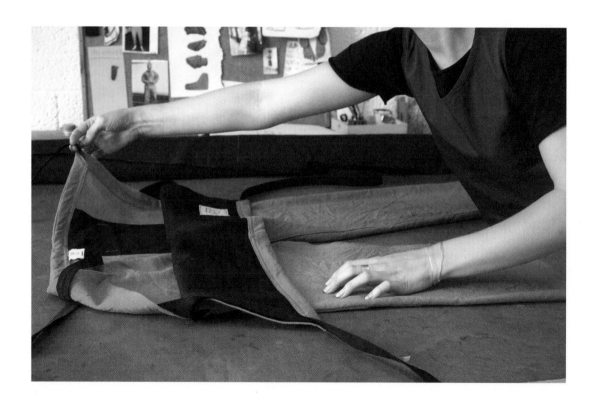

Sophie Woodrow

CERAMICIST

Sophie is a Bristolian. She grew up in the city and attended the Bristol Waldorf school, where she was fortunate to practice many different crafts including pottery, textiles and woodwork. This suited her creative sensibilities; she was always happiest when working with her hands and chose to pursue ceramics, which offered a balance between technique and expression – having some limitations almost offers more freedom.

Sophie moved to the Cornish town of Falmouth to pursue her studies in ceramics. Since then she has refined an intricate, labour-intensive technique and a highly distinctive visual language, simultaneously working on several pieces at once. It's a fairly slow process; each piece starts with a thumb pot, and the body is built from the bottom up, either coiling or using pieces of porcelain like a patchwork; textures and patterns are created with impressing or incising, sprigging or modelling, all sorts of methods. The head is the last part. Each piece is finished with a clear glaze, letting the form speak for itself without adding colour, which could add unnecessary meaning or metaphor. 'I remember when I was about fourteen I had made a pleasing but very heavy pot, a tutor said something to me about expanding the clay, giving it tension, like a pregnant belly. I think I understood something then about the vitality of the material that has stayed with me

Her work has been informed by an interest in the Victorians as the first generation who chose to define nature in opposition to what is human. In a spirit of wild curiosity, tinged with fear, the Victorians idolised nature, 'packaging' it into highly romanticised, palatable works of art. Our modern-day understanding is very different, so that we now interpret much Victorian art as 'unnatural' or kitsch.

Pursuing an interest in natural history, Sophie has looked particularly at our continually shifting theories of evolution. Her work has been inspired by the enormous misinterpretations of geological evidence made by the Victorians, often with bluff self-confidence, regarding these misinterpretations as a game of Chinese whispers played out over millennia. Sophie's sculptures are not visitors from other worlds, but the 'might-have-beens' of this world. She seeks to assemble creatures from the strange notions of what we define as 'nature' and of each other as people – as 'other'.

Inspiration comes in many forms, especially in the things she sees around her every day, such as the quality of light on different surfaces, the natural environment, the built environment, people and their peculiar ways, and most of all animals – how they live in our collective imaginations.

Moving back to Bristol after her degree was an easy decision for Sophie; it has the culture of a big city but without too much of the big-city stress. She had a romantic notion of living in London but after speaking to friends who moved there, that was put to rest.

For many years Sophie was based in a shared studio space at Jamaica Street Studios in Stokes Croft and BV Studios; this gave her the space and support structure that is essential after graduating. However, with a young family this became difficult, so she made the move to a studio at the bottom of her garden. Whilst only a few steps away from home, it is a world away; clad in an oversized fleece-lined boilersuit with digital radio in hand (the clay covered CD stack is long gone) she can focus entirely on her clay creatures. Sophie's studio is a large, light-filled, double-height space with plants of all shapes and sizes dotted around, porcelain creatures peeking out through the leaves and flowers. The space feels like a place one can escape to and create all day long, as well as being her children's very own Hobbit home!

When it's time to escape the studio, Sophie enjoys a stroll through the huge park near her home in East Bristol that leads to the River Frome, where you can walk for miles. Getting outside everyday is an important routine; it's always uplifting and motivating. A visit to Clifton to sample the shops, cafes and beautiful surrounds is also an occasional treat. 'Bristol allows me the freedom to feel that what I do is possible; there are so many other people choosing to make their living from a creative business, that's inspiring and encouraging.'

Whilst Sophie is able to sell much of her work online through her website, taking part in exhibitions and fairs is something she hopes to do more of as it offers the opportunity to meet and converse with other creatives, necessary when working from a solitary studio. That said, Sophie doesn't struggle with cabin fever; rather, she has become accustomed to and reliant on the quiet reflective time that making gives her. Ceramics can be relaxing and cathartic for many people and is perhaps the main reason why there has been a surge in its popularity as a hobby recently. People want to find a way of 'switching off', using their hands and not their minds for a while.

A recent high point in her practice was the opportunity for Sophie to exhibit with Claire Curneen and Christie Brown in a group exhibition at Messums Wiltshire titled 'Material Earth: Myth, Material and Metamorphosis'. They were the idols of her student days, both drawing from narrative to create otherworldly sculptures. Whilst Sophie's children are young, projects are fairly spaced out; however, she does have a few ideas on the backburner and something quite different in form and size to the small figurative pieces she has become known for. Her studio could soon become a forest to larger creatures!

www.sophiewoodrow.co.uk

Stephanie Tudor

VISUAL ARTIST

Stephanie is a multidisciplinary artist producing sculptural installations and bespoke furniture. A childhood spent in rural Wiltshire instilled a passion for creative play and making things with her hands; mud pies, whittling sticks and crafting leafy dens were commonplace. 'So much of my inspiration and drive comes from the natural environment. Not just the pretty things, but the raw and dirty things too. Bringing overlooked materials to the fore makes you appreciate them in a different way.'

Her practice is materials and process led, focusing on the exploration of tactility and surface quality; she is interested in the emotional response materials can evoke and the relationship that occurs between object and audience, seeking to strengthen connections through touch. Inspired by naturally occurring textures, the work combines found, organic and reclaimed elements, from slate fallen from rooftops, chips of rusted iron and derelict gates to moss found in soggy gutters.

Stephanie's degree in Textile Design at Central Saint Martins was broad enough that she was able to experiment with surface design and mixed media material outcomes rather than textiles in a traditional sense, and her tutors were supportive of her chosen direction.

After graduating, Stephanie spent several months in Holland working with artist Nacho Carbonell, where she learnt the ins and outs of running a successful creative business. On returning to the UK she fairly quickly discovered In Bristol Studio and immediately knew it was the place for her to grow and develop her creative practice. Based in an old cotton mill, the studio complex is split into thirty individual spaces with shared facilities such as a wood workshop, print and ceramics room. Being amongst such a vast group of creatives has certainly influenced her work and taught her an array of practical skills that were not immediately available at university. 'It feels like a mini art college sometimes, and there's always more than one person making something big and messy.'

Stephanie enjoys the freedom that comes with being self-employed and embraces the challenges it brings, using it as a driver to move forward. You have to be flexible and ride the wave in order not to sink as a self-employed creative, which seems to come naturally to Stephanie, although she admits her organisational skills are lacking – a constant source of irritation for her.

Having the space and freedom to create bigger work means there is no limit to the materials she gathers on her walks in the countryside, collecting bits of earth, twigs and seed pods along the way, marvelling at their beauty and ingenuity. Stephanie merges found, organic and reclaimed materials into her work, including slate, rusted iron from old gates, moss and weeds from a hillside, creating a connection between the natural and man-made.

Experimenting with reclaimed materials is an important part of Stephanie's practice. She wants to evoke a sense of the natural world through the use of tactile materials or prompt people to think twice about 'waste' by bringing these elements to the fore and celebrating their unique qualities, from metal swarf from the drilling industry and broken shards from local glassblowers to terracotta bricks and rubble from building sites.

For inspiration, Stephanie researches the vibrant design and craft movement across the UK and internationally and the innovative grassroots approach to design in the European architecture and urban design scene. She looks to contemporaries such as Jo Lathwood, a Bristol-based artist who weaves wonderful narrative and processes into her work; Lola Lely, a London-based designer with an innovative, fresh approach, and Julian Watts, an American woodcarver who creates playful sculptures so full of character that you want them to be

your friends. Wonky ceramics, abstract painters, sculptors, furniture and urban designers all play a part in inspiring her day-to-day practice.

Like many of the designers featured in this book, Stephanie was part of Hothouse by Crafts Council, a programme of creative and business support for ambitious and talented new makers across the UK. Luckily for her, in the year she took part (2014) several other makers from Bristol were chosen (Angie Parker, Alex McCarthy, Anna Gravelle) and so many friendships were formed and they continue to offer support and advice to each other on a regular basis. Outside the studio, Stephanie regularly attends the many exhibitions and events at Spike Island and the Royal West of England Academy (RWA), two of Bristol's leading contemporary art galleries.

Since setting up her studio Stephanie works mostly on commissions, usually through word of mouth. Working on a broad range of individual and collaborative projects, including high-end furniture commissioned by The New Craftsmen, and more recently has been involved in community engagement projects with Studio Meraki, a collective of artists whose projects provide creative workshops to revive urban parks in Bristol.

In the future Stephanie is aiming to fuse the different areas of her creative practice together; the studio practice and the community work. Her dream is to create wild and wonderful structures with children and then translate them into sculptural pieces for outdoor public spaces, facilitating workshops that offer both a creative and educational opportunity.

www.stephanietudor.co.uk

Angie Parker

WEAVER

Angie Parker is an award-winning weaver of rugs and exquisite, vibrant textiles derived from traditional Scandinavian rug-weaving techniques. Her distinctive and intricate floor art and fabric creations are hand-woven using long established patterns, such as Krokbragd, which she combines with her instinctive and daring approach to colour. A year spent living in India and more recently the dynamic graffiti in her neighbourhood in Bristol have influenced the fabulously gaudy palette which is intrinsic to her weaving. Her colour spectrum ranges from intensely hued to eye-popping flamboyance and sourcing new shades is a key part of her planning.

Angie grew up in south Manchester with a gifted knitter and seamstress for a Mum and an engineering-minded Dad. This meant that making was commonplace in her life from an early age. A throw-away comment from Angie's secondary school art teacher, Juliet Caithness, about her natural flair for textiles gave her a nudge in the right direction.

The first time she actually used a loom, at Cumbria College of Art over twenty years ago, was a serendipitous moment in Angie's life; it felt like the perfect fit and moving forward she knew that weaving would play an important role in her career.

It is the creative process of importing a contemporary element to the time-honoured techniques of rug weaving and the responses from the viewer which most excite her. Her often ostentatious approach to design has evolved over the years, and whilst she is happy to adapt her work for private commissions, she is reluctant to rein it in for the one-off pieces she produces to exhibit and promote her practice. 'It was love that brought me to Bristol in 2003. I'd worked in the city on two previous occasions and something about the creative vibe made it stand out from all the other places I'd worked in. The third time here, I met the man who is now my unbelievably supportive and brilliant husband and dad to our three girls.'

In 2006 Angie had the opportunity to live in India due to her husband's job; initially it was to be for six months and at the time she was working freelance, so it felt like a now or never opportunity. Angie was based in Bangalore but travelled to Kerala, Mysore, Hampi, Goa and Ahmedabad during what became almost a year in India. She also volunteered at a school for deaf children and spent the rest of her days visiting galleries, markets and sari shops, drinking in the vibrant colour which surrounded her.

Her time spent in India had a profound influence on Angie's work and continues to play an important role in her practice; the 'Indiranagar designs' are inspired by this time.

Indiranagar is named after the Bangalore neighbourhood where Angie lived, itself named after the colourful first female Prime Minister of India, Indira Ghandi. The bold colours and pops of glitter represent the layering of colours in the sari shops she loved to visit, and the clashes of colour everywhere. As well as being inspired by the beautiful fabrics, Angie was in awe of the women she met whilst living in India, and through the Indiranagar range, Angie celebrates the life of one of India's most important women.

Working in reclaimed quality rug wool, Angie meticulously hand-weaves and finishes all the pieces herself on her huge Glimakra floor loom at BV Studios in Bedminster, a short walk from her home. Angie often talks about the influence of the graffiti in this area of Bristol and how it plays a role in her work; walking past a new piece on the way to the studio will often feed directly into whatever is on the loom.

It's Angie's genuine passion for what she does that keeps her going in the often challenging world of craft and design, alongside a determination to be successful in her chosen field; proving to her three daughters that through hard work it can be done. She admits that the logistics of earning a living from craft can get to her sometimes, but the second she gets on the loom that all fades away because she knows this is what she does best. 'Nothing is handed to you on a plate. Behind every single achievement and accolade is a shedload of planning and plain old hard graft.'

Angie's calendar is never dull; at the time of writing she is finishing preparations for a London Craft Week exhibition and will then be focusing on marketing her limited edition collection of rugs made from recycled plastic bottles. She has recently started to teach weaving workshops and is often booked to give talks on running a creative practice.

Angie is also a member of 'seam', a contemporary textile collective based in Bath and made up of a group of established embroiderers, printers, knitters, weavers, dyers, fashion designers, eco-designers, makers and artists who want to make textiles that are irresistible and find their way onto your body, into your house and onto your walls. They share a commitment to pushing the boundaries of their craft and making high quality objects realised in the hands and thoughts of the maker.

In the future, Angie would like to see her practice become more focused on creating textile artworks, and she acknowledges that creating commercial designs and products means her weaving can support her in achieving this goal. At the time of writing this profile, Angie has three exhibitions booked and is looking forward to helping people benefit from having more colour in their lives with her textiles.

www.angieparkertextiles.com

Libby Ballard

CERAMICIST

Libby grew up on the Isle of Wight, which has distilled a love for the English coastline and outdoors that clearly informs her practice as a ceramicist. The shades of blue layered on top of the flecked stoneware clay instantly take you to a warm sunny day at the seaside where the water and sky seamlessly blend into one another. This theme is carried throughout her hand-thrown work in the form of everyday tableware, planters and vases that sit quietly in any surrounding. 'I love taking pictures, and soaking in all the sounds and fresh sea air just makes me want to get on the wheel and make!'

Libby remained by the sea whilst studying for her degree in 3D Materials Practice at the University of Brighton, where contemporary porcelain ceramic artist Jo Davies was her tutor. After graduating in 2013, a year later, in 2014, Libby Ballard Ceramics was founded from a studio in London. However, after three years in London, Libby felt a growing desire to escape the city and move closer to the countryside and the coast. After much deliberation, Bristol was her choice and she hasn't looked back, basing herself at the Pound Arts Centre in Corsham just outside Bristol, where she has found a wonderful network of designers and artists within an engaging and proactive organisation.

Upon moving to Bristol, Libby engaged in a Prince's Trust enterprise course which has provided invaluable support to her. An intensive one-week business course armed her with the skills needed to run a business alongside ongoing mentoring sessions, events and marketing help, which gave Libby the boost she needed to go full-time with her work. She learnt certain lessons the hard way, in particular not to undervalue your work, and to use a system to price your work that reflects the cost of making and your time.

Libby spends long days in her studio completing orders, making new work, posting packages and teaching workshops alongside managing her own PR and social media that is so vital to growing businesses. There are not enough hours in the day and Libby has recently made the decision to employ someone one day a week to assist with the workload – a scary but necessary step for many makers.

Whilst in the studio, Radio 6 on in the background, Libby can settle in to what she loves most. Like many ceramicists Libby enjoys the labour-intensive nature of making with clay; the process begins with wedging the clay, blending two different stoneware clays together and

then weighing out balls of clay to throw with. Each piece is then individually thrown on the wheel and left overnight to harden. The bases are then tidied up and any handles will be added. The pieces are then left to completely dry for up to a week and then bisque fired. Pieces are then glazed in Libby's own unique glaze recipes that are mixed up from a selection of ingredients. The bases are then wiped of any glaze and fired again to 1,260 degrees. It takes between two and three weeks for each piece to be completed. 'I love that you can reuse a piece of clay again and again until you come up with ideas that work.'

Libby's day varies depending on whether she is completing wholesale orders, one-off commissions or running a workshop. Teaching is an aspect of her practice Libby loves and hopes to continue in the future, spending one day a week running workshops for the growing community of hobbyist potters. There has been a surge in demand in Bristol and throughout the UK with people wanting to take up pottery as a hobby or to turn it into a full-time practice; programmes such as *The Great Pottery Throwdown* have certainly boosted this trend, alongside

many people's desire to reconnect with their creative self and switch off from the faster pace and instant gratification of social media and television.

Libby makes the most of what Bristol has to offer in the form of food, gigs and art whilst being close to the countryside and coastlines of Cornwall and Devon has obvious advantages – offering fresh inspiration to inform her ceramic practice and passion for photography, walking and camping. Within just a couple of years living and working in Bristol, Libby has found the city to be a thriving place for designer/makers, offering many opportunities for networking, support and outlets to promote and sell her work, and taking part in local markets such as the Bristol Etsy events.

Bristol has become a hotspot for food – new cafes and food trends pop-up on what seems a weekly basis. Libby has taken inspiration from this and reflected on how she can make her collections more functional, becoming part of everyday use within the home. She believes there is a much bigger appetite for the handmade in Bristol compared to London; perhaps in part due to Bristol being a forward-thinking city with a rebellious nature, there is a desire to own items that have a unique imprint rather than off-the-shelf mass-produced things. Bristol also loves coffee and has a new festival – the Coffee House Project – where Libby sold a new range of travel cups in 2018. Working as a designer/maker can be a lonely task and so collaborating on projects and commissions is a rewarding aspect of any maker's practice.

www.libbyballard.co.uk

Liz Vidal

CERAMICIST

Liz creates functional ceramics and unique one-off pieces using stoneware or porcelain. She is inspired by the idea that her pots become a part of someone's daily ritual, whether that be as their favourite bowl for breakfast or first choice of mug for their morning coffee. The sense that their owners build relationships with these objects, which in time hold memories and emotions for them, fascinates Liz. 'My Dad is a joiner and I always admired his ability to transform pieces of wood into functional and beautiful items with his hands.'

Sitting at her pottery wheel in her studio just north of Bristol, Liz describes the mindful process of making her pots. Each piece starts as a lump of clay which is wedged, weighed and divided into balls for throwing. After a piece is thrown on the wheel it's left to dry for a day or two until it's 'leather hard' but still soft enough to trim the bottom or attach a handle. The pots are then left to completely dry out before firing to 1,000 degrees in her electric kiln. Once fired, they are unloaded and glazed in Liz's unique colour combinations before being re-fired. Two days later the kiln is opened to reveal a treasure trove of beautiful pots; from matt speckled plates to glossy turquoise mugs, it's a delight for the senses!

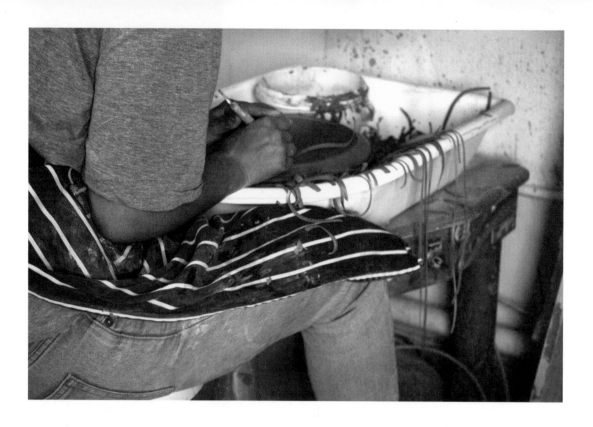

Having grown up in Kent, Liz moved to Manchester to attend university. Studying Three-Dimensional Design at Manchester School of Art was the beginning of her journey into functional ceramics and led to an apprenticeship at North Street Potters in London. Here Liz learnt the ins and outs of running a successful studio and taught herself to throw. She sees this time as the most significant in her career and soon began to make ranges of tableware for restaurants, including Coya in Mayfair, and Fera at Claridge's. Throwing hundreds and hundreds of small ceviche bowls was great practice and the sales of these pots was the perfect way to save for an adventure overseas.

An urge to experience new cultures and their relationship with ceramics inspired Liz to look for opportunities outside of the UK and immerse herself in a new world of pottery. This urge took Liz to the Gaya Ceramic Art Centre in Ubud, Bali, where she spent six months interning. She taught pottery classes to expats, learnt how to wood fire, helped run the studio and became skilled in sgraffito, sometimes spending days perfecting the decoration on one plate. After her internship Liz travelled for another twelve months, during which time she undertook a

residency with Renton Bishopric, a potter on the Sunshine Coast in Australia. Renton's studio is an old horse stable with no proper doors, a resident 7ft python in the rafters and no running water – a stark contrast to the workspaces she was used to. When returning to the UK, London felt too hectic and the creative buzz of Bristol was a massive draw. It seemed the perfect location to grow a small business within a supportive artistic community.

Liz lives in the city but works at Hillside Studios, which are located in the countryside on the outskirts of Bristol, with a view out towards the Severn Bridge and Wales. Originally a pigsty, it seemed as good a place as any to create a mess! She was looking for a space that would allow her to make as well as teach. Set in a meadow with several other studios housing artists, with her doors open to the wild flowers, trees and a freshwater dipping pool, Liz has certainly found the idyllic creative space. Whilst working in Australia, where Renton's workshop overlooked Mount Coolum, Liz realised how much having a view can influence your productivity and mood. Being close to nature is important to her and driving out to the studio in the calming countryside always eases her into the day ahead. Liz also draws inspiration from visiting the green spaces in the city, including the Downs or the beautiful meadows of South Purdown. She loves that in Bristol you are never too far away from a spectacular view.

Liz is currently producing work for a variety of local restaurants and shops including Poco Tapas in Stokes Croft, and Two Belly on Whiteladies Road. With a style that has been described as rustic and fresh, she plans to continue creating handmade wares for local homes and businesses. As with all crafts, there is such a rich history in ceramics and many avenues to explore, whether it be a different firing technique or new form to throw, Liz hopes to never stop learning.

www.lizvidalceramics.com

Anna Gravelle

TEXTILE ARTIST

Anna is a textile artist and designer, producing embellished fabrics for domestic interiors and public spaces. Working within craft and digital processes, Anna creates luxurious wall art and a range of interior furnishing fabrics and accessories that combine print and surface embellishment.

Anna is Welsh and grew up in Cardiff; she can recount several early memories of specific textiles that made an impact on her. The *brethyn* (the Welsh word for woollen cloth) in particular stands out and is made into capes, purses, school uniforms and the obligatory Welsh national costume; it is a scratchy fabric that anyone growing up in Wales will not forget easily. At home Anna had tufted chenille candlewick bedspreads, handmade Trevira trousers and knitted tabards, all courtesy of Anna's mum, who taught her how to sew and knit. 'My mind was set from the age of about fifteen that I wanted to go to art college and so I focused on making that happen.'

Anna pursued a Fine Art degree at Cardiff Art College back in the 1980s and focussed on film-making, performance and installation art. Following college she worked in the television industry for sixteen years, originally making pop videos for Welsh bands and then arts and music documentaries for the BBC, which coincided with a move to Bristol. 'I travelled a lot, met great people and loved all the fascinating locations that television production offered, but was frustrated with making programmes by committee. I craved creative autonomy and a return to hands-on making.'

After several years at the BBC, Anna longed to be making with her hands again – she had an inkling that textiles was the way forward and so enrolled on a short course in textile printing at Central Saint Martins in London and after just a few weeks decided to jump ship from the BBC to carve out a new career. Anna then completed an MA in Textile Design at Bath Spa University, which solidified her direction and is where she first came across the tufting machine that has become her trademark technique.

Anna established her Bristol studio in 2013. Working within craft and digital processes she creates luxurious wall art alongside a range of interior furnishing fabrics and accessories that combine print and surface embellishment. Texture is at the heart of her design process, with the aim of creating a beguiling and unexpected tactile experience within domestic interiors and public settings. 'I have made my home in Bristol with my family. We are tenants on a National Trust estate on the fringes of Bristol. It would be difficult to leave.'

Anna was selected for the Crafts Council's prestigious Hothouse programme for emerging designer/makers in 2014 and was nominated for the Perrier-Jouët Arts Salon Prize in 2015. The South West cohort at Hothouse had a strong bond from the offset and many of them moved to Bristol and remain good friends; they are a real lifeline for Anna as she works in isolation from her garden studio. She also has a strong network of fellow designers and practitioners she has met at trade fairs and from lecturing at art colleges.

Anna spends a lot of her spare time looking at art, craft and design exhibitions and flicking through interiors or architectural magazines; the spaces featured in the magazines are often a great starting point for a design. There are always new things to discover, to try and to make. New patterns, different colour palettes, effects to create – that's what drives the process forward day to day. But for Anna the greatest satisfaction is when a piece she has designed and made is completed and she gets to deliver it to its new owner.

Ambitions for the future lie in creating bespoke commissions alongside new product developments and industry collaborations. Anna really enjoys working with clients to produce bespoke textiles for their homes and would like to extend that offer to public spaces.

The hard edges of a building plus the potential to also soften the acoustics of a public space. Recently she has been collaborating with an acoustic panel manufacturer to produce a range of bespoke panels with a more handcrafted feel. For someone who used to direct music videos this is an exciting prospect. Music is Anna's second love but she doesn't spend as much time playing as she used to; the reality of running a creative business, being a mum and teaching, means there isn't much time left for hobbies!

Inspiration comes in many guises: the natural landscape and gardens Anna has on her doorstep alongside museums and galleries, in particular Bristol Museum and Art Gallery. When her daughter was much younger, they spent a lot of time studying the stuffed animals in the 'still zoo', the fossils and geological samples, and the vast collection of Modernist artworks they have there.

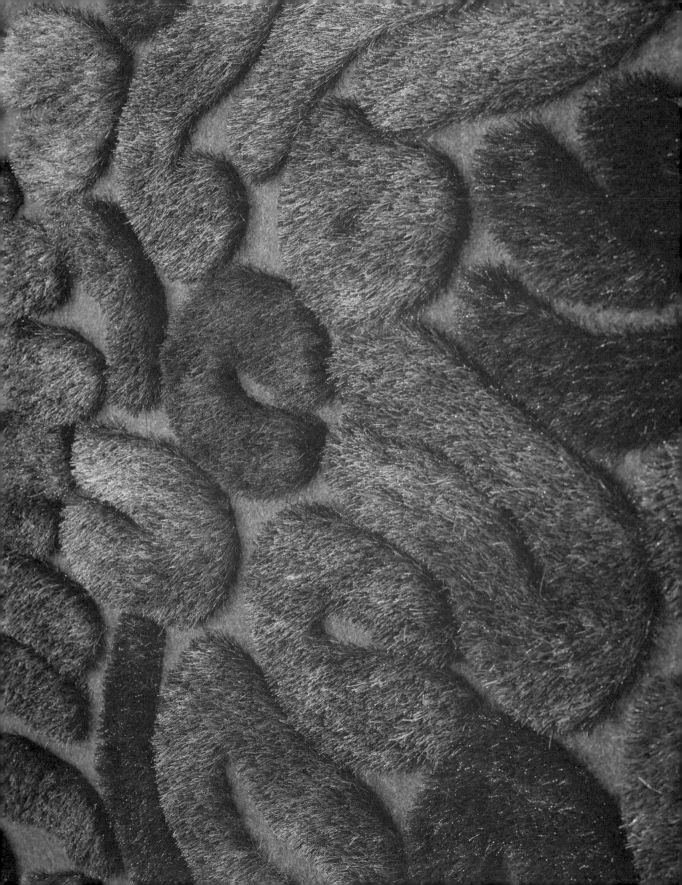

Recently Anna discovered the work of Simone Meulpin at the 'Collect' exhibition in London and was blown away buy her textile sculptures and wall panels; she builds the pieces by folding and pinning white cotton fabric into exquisite forms – it's not until you get up close that you see the materials and techniques used. Anna also adore's Laura Ellen Bacon's willow sculptures; they are like three-dimensional drawings and the site-specific pieces act like textural interventions pushing out of buildings or flowing through the landscape.

www.annagravelle.com

Amber Hards

KNITWEAR DESIGNER

Amber is interested in producing innovative and beautiful knitwear, experimenting with contrasting yarns and techniques that produce unexpected garments with texture, volume and movement.

Growing up in both town and country (Leicester and Cumbria), Amber was instantly taken by Bristol's Bower Ashton Campus that straddles the city but is surrounded by lovely countryside. Amber completed both her foundation diploma in Art and Design and BA Hons in Fashion and Textiles there nine years ago and has remained in Bristol ever since. Falling in love with both the city and a Bristolian have played a large part in this, but so have the friends and creative network she has gained since completing her foundation and degree courses.

Over the twelve years of living and working in Bristol, Amber has bonded with a strong network of individuals working within her field of fashion and knit which has proven invaluable. She has friends working as stylists, make-up artists, photographers, designers and knitters to collaborate on projects and who offer her feedback when needed.

Amber previously had a space at BV Studios in Bedminster but when she decided to go full-time with her own brand in 2016 it made sense to work from home. This offers Amber more flexibility and allows her to save some money each month – which can feel like such a relief, especially when making the transition to work full-time on your own brand. Working on knitting machines from her small back room allows Amber to do a bit of work whenever she feels like it – pyjamas to boot. Working from home can be quite isolating, so Amber often breaks up the day by doing her admin work at The Assembly in Old Market, passing by various independent shops and pop-ups from other local designers on the way.

A normal day for Amber usually starts with some yoga, helping to calm her mind and focus on the day ahead. Lauren Laverne on Radio 6 follows soon after and Amber is in her zone, completely transfixed by the process of knitting. Amber's passion for her craft shines through with leaps and bounds; it is all-consuming and inspiring to watch. Like a magpie, she is drawn to visual stimulus through ceramics, weaving, embroidery, paintings, photographs, animation and theatre; finding inspiration and the opportunity to translate that into knit is an exciting proposition to her.

For inspiration Amber often heads to The Wardrobe Theatre or the Central Library – the reference library upstairs offers a grand theatrical quality. Nature plays a dominant role in Amber's creations and so spaces and places that can trigger her imagination are always welcome such as Bristol Museum, which houses a spectacular collection of butterflies. Closer to home a stroll through St George's Park often hits the mark. 'I love texture so anything in nature from plants, animals, rock formations can inspire me and inform fabrics from form, movement, texture, pattern. And what is more beautiful than nature?'

Aside from nature, fellow fashion designers provide inspiration for Amber's research. The man who kick-started her passion for fashion was the late Alexander McQueen, whose creations explored the use of fabric to the extreme. In terms of her contemporaries she looks to designers such as Mark Fast – who was a great inspiration to her throughout university and opened Amber's eyes to what knitwear can be – and Matty Bovan, whose designs remind Amber to trust her instincts and not over-think her work. Closer to home, the Bristol Textile Quarter offers support to a diverse group of creatives while the Bristol Weaving Mill encourages textile production to take place in the UK.

Amber teaches machine-knitting workshops from her home studio and at the Bristol Textile Quarter. These workshops are brilliant for both beginners who want to try something new and students wanting to get a great headstart in their fashion textile degrees. Amber multitasks to the extreme; including teaching, freelancing, designing and making her collections. Her aim is to focus solely on her own collections, producing two a year, designed and made in Bristol, and to continue using British fibres; she currently sources lambswool from a small family-run company in Yorkshire. For her current collection, Amber is looking into the textures, shapes, movement and history of flamingos to create new fabrics and silhouettes, with a desire to add embroidery, print and fabric manipulation. A dream commission would be to create an outfit for Bjork – this seems an obvious muse for her creations which are ethereal, playful and theatrical all at once. 'I have a wonderful quote from Picasso on my studio wall: "Inspiration exists but it must find you working". I love the idea that inspiration is its own entity, that it'll find you, but you must be making work already in order for it to happen.'

At the moment, Amber's work is sold online through her own website and occasionally at markets, which give her the opportunity to showcase her tactile work in person – sales go up when people can actually touch the work and see the quality of each piece. Finding stockists is an ongoing but necessary task for Amber, the clothes need to be in a physical shop where they can be tried on and admired; seeing them on an actual person gives the work a whole new dimension.

www.amberhards.co.uk

Catriona R. MacKenzie

GLASSBLOWER

Catriona's work is bold and full of texture, uplifting in her use of colour combinations and clean shapes. She enjoys the layering qualities that glassblowing encourages and uses colour techniques and glass carving to create three-dimensional worlds within each form.

Her inspiration come from the world around her, and the sanctuary she finds within certain environments – walking in the woods in her native Scotland, or sitting having a coffee next to the graffiti of Bristol. She enjoys the juxtaposition of these different themes, and uses opposites throughout her work. This can evolve from a contrasting colour or surface texture, to the use of light and the obscuring of light. 'By using opaque-coloured glass I can convince the viewer that they are looking at a piece of glazed porcelain. Only when they realise that the interior of the piece is transparent does the material reveal itself to be blown glass. I like carving through the layer of opaque colour to create these "windows" into the interior world within.'

Catriona was born in Glasgow, but grew up in the Scottish Highlands. Her desire to capture the visual world was there from a very young age, with her interest in becoming a designer and maker being nurtured as she honed her skills in college and university. She loves getting caught up in the process of making, and has spent the last seventeen years honing her technique.

Catriona studied a degree in Design and Applied Arts, specialising in Glass and Architectural Glass at Edinburgh College of Art (ECA), and as an exchange student at Alfred University, New York State, USA for six months. While at the ECA, she also studied Jewellery as a second subject.

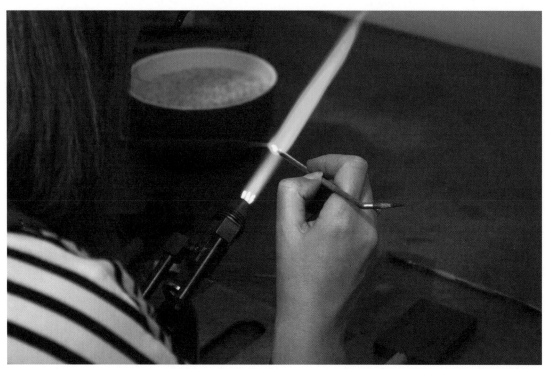

She then went on to study a two-year postgraduate diploma in blown and carved glass at the prestigious International Glass Centre (IGC), West Midlands. The IGC really pushed Catriona's skill levels, and she came away with an extensive knowledge.

One of Catriona's favourite glassblowers is Tobias Mohl. His work is highly complex cane work, but very simple beautiful shapes. She completed a masterclass with him and Janusz Pozniak at North Lands Creative in 2008; working together on designs and making a final product.

After her education, Catriona then went on to work as a full-time glassblower and studio manager in a very busy studio in the Cotswolds. Her four years in this position taught her other essential skills including how to run a craft business, training staff, and working to tight timeframes. During this time she was selected to exhibit a series of her own work at COLLECT 2011, which professionally was a fantastic experience for Catriona.

At the end of 2011, Catriona moved to Bristol due to medical complications following an operation. Being tenacious and forward-thinking, she spent the following three years of her rehabilitation to focus entirely on her own practice; she refreshed her jewellery-making skills

in her box room and attended jewellery courses at Flux Gallery in Bristol. She also returned to lampwork glass. Bristol soon became an important creative home for Catriona and she began to be influenced by the environment around her. 'I love it here. I have lots of ties with friends, creative circles, and I just like the vibe the city has. The coast and the countryside is also very important to me, and I like the fact I can get away to it quite easily.'

Catriona won the Silver Award for Glass from the *Craft & Design Magazine* in 2013 and she was also a finalist in 2014 and 2016. In 2015, Catriona was awarded a place on the Crafts Council's Hothouse 5 mentoring programme. This invaluable knowledge has boosted her own business and helped her gain a large network of friends and fellow makers in Bristol and the South West. In 2017 Catriona was successful in obtaining a studio space within the distinguished Centrespace Studios, Bristol's longest running artist studio space.

Being run as a co-operative, each creative business based there plays a role in the management, which is what attracted Catriona to begin with. The space is situated next to the popular St Nick's Market, so it acts as a great base for Catriona to offer beginners' bead-making classes.

Nature is an important element in Catriona's work and whilst she loves Bristol, the Highlands are her home and feature quite subtly in most of her work. Day to day there are plenty of opportunities to soak up some countryside views and be at one with nature; wandering around one of Bristol's many parks or taking in the city from Ashton Court or Clifton Downs. It recharges the batteries and sparks new ideas. 'I have a keen interest in mycology and myxomycetes, so these feature heavily in my work. It ties in a lot with my love of nature and being from the Highlands of Scotland. Walking in the woods is a sanctuary to me.'

Catriona sources her glass colour from UK suppliers, who stock from various companies, mostly in Europe or New Zealand. Her unique jeweller's hallmark is from Edinburgh Assay Office, sticking to her Scottish roots, and where she first studied jewellery, under Dorothy Hogg MBE at the ECA. Day to day tasks and teaching is carried out at her Centrespace Studio with the radio on and a cup of tea in hand, but if glassblowing is on the agenda it entails a 6 a.m. start, beginning with a two-hour drive north to Stourbridge Glassblowing Studio. Starting at 9 a.m. it's a nonstop day of making until closing time. The next day, once everything has cooled down to room temperature, Catriona can begin to grind and polish the bases or do any carving needed on the pieces.

Catriona is currently working on various exhibitions, including one she will be curating herself and including other contemporary makers. She is also designing new ranges of both her glassware and jewellery, and collaborating with other makers who use different materials. One constant always remains throughout Catriona's work – that there will be colour.

www.catmackglass.com

Charlotte Duckworth

SILVERSMITH

Charlotte designs and makes beautiful cutlery from sterling silver and locally sourced English holly, creating functional pieces of art for the kitchen under her brand name The Silver Duck. Her ethos revolves around simple, elegant designs that are ergonomic and tactile, with the intention of provoking people to appreciate their food and take time over their daily routines and rituals in the kitchen. Preserving and capturing the natural qualities of the materials used, Charlotte creates magical utensils with a rugged, native feel to them. Her pieces are designed to function, with appreciation towards the natural beauty and proportion between the materials.

Her work has fine details and is finished to a high standard. Hallmarked in London in accordance to the Assay Office's rules and regulations.

Nature is the overriding inspiration for Charlotte's work and immersing herself in the creative process is a daily task: foraging for branches that fit the designs by jumping through hedgerows and stomping around woods. Bristol has some lovely walks to enable this. Trees, plants and flowers will always be the stimulation and provocation within her design process.

Tools shops, workshops and art shops also have their part to play in what inspires and influences her. Of her contemporaries, Charlotte admires the work of Brett Payne; he creates wonderfully balanced work where the display becomes part of the performance. Zoe Watts creates beautiful forms with incredible detail and Lasse Baehring makes tableware and other functional objects.

Charlotte has won various awards in recognition of her work, from an award from the National Association of Decorative and Fine Arts Societies (NADFAS) in 2013 to winning the Best New Talent Award in 2015 and the LUX Global Excellence award – British Silversmiths of the Year 2017 and Excellence Award for Sterling Silver Cutlery Production 2017. She has also received various mentoring from institutions such as the Crafts Council's Hothouse mentoring programme and Goldsmiths' Company graduate mentoring for Goldsmiths' Fair. 'I have a keen interest in mycology and myxomycetes, so these feature heavily in my work. It ties in a lot with my love of nature and being from the Highlands of Scotland. Walking in the woods is a sanctuary to me.'

Charlotte grew up in Devon and the Highlands of Scotland, spending her student days in Buckinghamshire before returning home to Devon for two years, saving money and learning how to drive, before deciding it was time to be part of a creative community again. She looked at several places to live including Sheffield, London and Staffordshire. Workshops she had

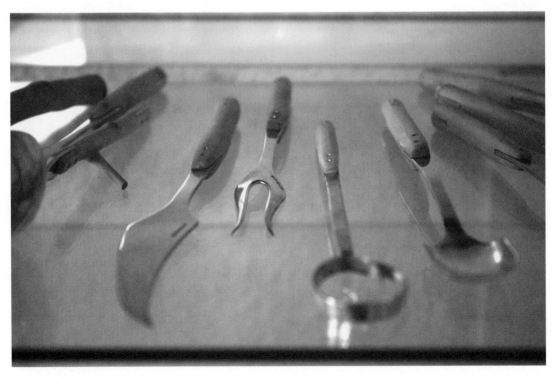

applied for either weren't quite right or fell through due to not being able to make specific dates for interviews, and so she was left with Bristol as the main option. Many friends from college had moved to the city when she was in Buckinghamshire, and she had also taken part in the Hothouse mentoring scheme run by Crafts Council and therefore had made connections with makers in and around the city; so it all seemed to fit into place.

Charlotte's studio is in Old Market Manor; they provide an affordable solution for those who require workshop or studio space by giving designer/makers access to temporary and permanent bench spaces. Building up her own workshop has been a slow process, starting in her living room and growing into the studio space, slowly building on her repertoire of tools; acquiring tools is one of her favourite hobbies, in league with collecting plants.

Her workshop is her safe-haven and her second home. Spending most days in the workshop, including the weekends, Charlotte is dedicated to what she does, and is constantly developing and practicing her techniques. Being in a multi-disciplined workshop has been a great benefit to Charlotte, and having steel fabricators and woodworkers in her vicinity greatly helps and improves her work. Her aim is to set up a jewellery studio in Bristol to create a jewellery network and supportive environment. She wants there to be space to teach students – both the public and people in the trade.

Charlotte is currently learning to turn bowls for a cake stand design she is making called the French Fancy Collection. This includes a three-tier cake stand, with dishes made from wood, joined together with silver. There are four plates made in a similar fashion with four pastry forks to complete the collection. It is no small undertaking! She is also looking to make some of her pieces in steel to lower costs and appeal to a different market, to be showcased at the end of the year.

Charlotte has also started designing and making chef serving collections including a serving spoon, a straining spoon and a saucier spoon, as well as measuring spoons and a carvery set. Having met Heston Blumenthal at Fairford Christmas Market, he is now the proud owner of her Tea Strainer and Sugar Pot. Her dream would be to work in partnership with a recognised chef to create specific pieces for them; a whole set of cutleries for an eight–twelve place settings. This would be a major undertaking, costing thousands of pounds to complete.

Charlotte has recently undertaken a commission for an exhibition for Michael Wignall, a two-star Michelin chef based in Devon. She created a Canape Serving Platter under the inspiration of Michael and the food he creates. This piece was different from the cutlery Charlotte usually makes, though it still has strong aesthetics linking to cutlery and utensil-based implements.

Charlotte has taken part in many prestigious exhibitions, such as Goldsmiths' Fair, Art in Action, Collect, and Henley Festival, and has her work represented in the USA and Europe. Being part of organisational bodies such as Contemporary British Silversmiths, Heritage Crafts Association, The Devon Guild, and Who's Who in Gold and Silver, Charlotte is recognised for her craft and regularly keeps up to date with opportunities she can partake in.

At the time of writing Charlotte has part-time jobs to help pay the bills, but she hopes to focus solely on her practice and run workshops from the studio to subsidise it. She currently teaches workshops at Flux in Bristol during the weekdays and at New Brewery Arts in Cirencester on weekends, also being hired by JASSO in Oxfordshire to run a workshop for their members, and holding a pop-up workshop in Kingston with West Elm.

www.thesilverduck.com

Jacky Puzey

DIGITAL EMBROIDERER

Jacky Puzey is a digital embroiderer of new fabrics, textures and stories; specialising in designing and producing embroidery for interiors and fashion.

Combining traditional embroidery skills with digital technology, Jacky uses fur, feathers, tweed and organza with drawings, laser cuttings and digital embroidery to explore her distinctive imagery and style. From feral lace to embellished creatures, feathered interior screens to shimmering metallic bomber jackets, Jacky's embroidery creates a baroque pleasure; forming new fabrics, textures and stories. 'I find new graffiti or traces of urban wildlife when I'm out running in Easton. I love going on urban walks or pottering around areas of Bristol looking for new or unusual things, from exhibitions to street art to foods to films to fashion to second-hand treasures.'

Jacky had an adventurous start to life; she grew up travelling around the world following her father's work for a big overseas bank. With her family she lived in Madrid, Antwerp, Milan, Panama City and she also visited her father in New York, Freetown Sierra Leone, Cameroon and Kenya. Her creativity came through from a young age, particularly painting and making things with her mum.

Eventually, Jacky settled in the UK to study Fine Art at Sheffield Hallam University and in 2005 moved to Bristol to become the Exhibitions Organiser at Watershed Media Centre, and was curator by the time she left after a serious accident in 2000. Throughout this period Jacky also studied for a postgraduate diploma in Visual Culture at Bath Spa University, where she researched digital cultures and technologies. This was preceded by an MA in Visual Culture (sculpture, textile print, hand embroidery, pattern cutting) and a PhD at Bath Spa University with her thesis 'Hybrid Dialogues, Situational Strategies: producing postcolonial visual cultures'. 'Resilience and adaptability is key and you need to learn to love the business balance too, or get appropriate help, for example from an accountant or an assistant. Be really careful to keep the focus on what is key for your business and your creative happiness together.'

Conceptually, Jacky explores a visual collaboration across cultures, from multicultural graffitied contemporary cityscapes to historical textiles. The embroidered artworks create a tension between bespoke craftsmanship and digital technologies, political concept and artistic form. Her current interiors collection features a series of interior products, from statement embroidered cocktail chairs, footstools and interior screens, to embroidered wallpapers.

Migrating creatures, from escaped parakeets to foxes and hares, are shown within their new urban landscapes to create a beautiful meditation on 'wild' cities and diverse urban cultures. The hare drinks from a forgotten corner of the pond in the park, camping out in a semi-public space. Parakeets mingle with the local starlings across an embroidered printed fabric screen. Koi carp stream over a forgotten urban graffitied river, from Japanese tradition to contemporary tattoo. Peacocks are embellished with contemporary henna designs and printed peonies. The embroideries bring alive shifting cultural allegiances to create complex contemporary embellished narratives of urban migration and landscape. The pieces are inspired by both the detail and depth of nineteenth-century landscape painting, and the desire to reflect twenty-first-century urban landscapes.

Jacky's inspiration comes from many forms, all relating to textiles: textile history, fashion, art, historical embellishment, street fashion, tailoring, postcolonial histories, photography, wearable technology, architecture, furniture and upholstery. She looks to the work of Karen Nicol, whose embroidery is incredibly creative and beautiful,and Allyson McDermott's wallpapers; she combines traditional and conservation techniques with new contemporary designs and did all the chinoiserie papers for the Brighton Pavilion; and the work of Tracy Kendall, whose wallpapers combine some extraordinary papers and has established a successful brand selling bespoke commissioned wallpapers.

Jacky lives and works in Easton; a creative, vibrant and diverse area of Bristol. Her studio is at Spaceworks, in the old Co-operative on Chelsea Road. She is part of a small network of other designers she collaborates with including Leigh-Anne Treadwell of Bristol Upholstery Collective, and stockist Whittaker Wells. She is also a member of Design Nation, and took part in the Crafts Council hothouse scheme. Jacky regularly shows with some of her Crafts Council Hothouse scheme associates, most recently as Collective Invites, at 67 York Street, London. 'It's so great to see all of our work develop and gain more exposure, from Hannah Townsend's amazing ceramics to Byron and Gomez's gorgeous furniture. To me it's important to look at practitioners at all stages of their career and to think about how to develop your own work and keep the buzz and enjoyment.'

Jacky is busy working on a wide variety of projects, including a new wallpaper collaboration with a Bath-based studio and planning a show with Design Nation at Eunique Karlsruhe, Nexus Exhibition with Fife Contemporary and Ruthin Crafts Centre and a collaborative embroidered banner for Processions project (Artichoke) with Lakes Alive Cumbria project group, alongside embroidered church banners for Kingston All Saints' Church in Kingston-on-Thames. Last

but not least, a range of embroidered cushions for a Jordanian client and a wedding dress embellishment using conductive thread for an American client.

Jacky's dream commission would be to work with either the V&A or the National Trust to produce an embroidered room; wallpapers, furnishings, etc. with access to their archives for research. Intrigued by eighteenth- and nineteenth-century scenic wallpapers, she enjoys shifting the landscape and chinoiserie tradition into something more contemporary.

www.jackypuzey.com

Oliver Cross and Lucy Lloyd

FOOTWEAR DESIGNERS

Ottowin Footwear was founded by couple Lucy Lloyd and Oliver (Ollie) Cross in 2016. It was born out of a love for traditional footwear craft, contemporary design and a great respect for their chosen material, leather. Their designs draw influence from traditional, wearable, everyday styles featuring sculptural contours and bold colours. They use colour to lighten the tone of the footwear, creating playful collections. Ottowin shoes are made to last, using luxury leather that ages beautifully; each pair has been on a journey from raw material to a stamped and signed Ottowin shoe. Ottowin is a meeting of minds and names; a combination of Lucy's nickname for Ollie 'Otto' and Ollie's nickname for Lucy 'Winnie', together creating Ottowin. 'We predominantly use industry waste leather for the uppers of our footwear – hand-selecting every hide to create beautiful useful objects from what would otherwise deteriorate and be thrown away.'

Through their brand they are promoting and providing 'slow fashion'; using their knowledge of materials to inform their decisions with the design and production. The vegetable tanned leather used to make each insole comes from Thomas Ware & Sons est. 1840; one of the only remaining traditional veg tanneries left in the UK, based just down the road along the River Avon in Bedminster.

This complete engagement with their product is something they have carried over into their own shop, which opened May 2018 on St Nicholas Street in the centre of Bristol. The Ottowin Shop was created after many conversations with small brands who have strong values and make beautiful products all based in the UK. These conversations formed the catalyst for Lucy and Ollie, who found a lovely space in a busy bustling part of town that is popular with creatives and the IT crowd alike, a curated haven of handmade eco-conscious fashion and homewares from local designer/makers including oB wear, Pico Project, Tamay and Me and Jessie Rose McGuinnness amongst others. Surrounding themselves with other creatives obviously plays an enormous role in their success and the drive to keep chasing their ideas and ideals; working closely with young brands, seeing them grow and flourish alongside Ottowin gives them a shared confidence and certainty in their work.

After studying at Cordwainers, London College of Fashion Lucy went on to work for an independent London-based footwear company, where she was head designer and managed overseas production and logistics for three years. Lucy gained valuable experience in the industry, but also became disenfranchised with the method of production and high turnover typical of

globalised manufacturing, which contributes to large amounts of waste. This experience was part of the driving force behind founding Ottowin, in which both Lucy and Oliver share the belief and can actively promote small-scale slow fashion. 'Bristol has a thriving scene of young independent makers – there is a creative freedom here which we haven't found in many places, there is space to create. The access to the countryside is a major reason, too – we love being able to get away and be immersed in nature within a short cycle or drive from where we live.'

Oliver comes from a fine art and design background. After graduating from university, he formed a collective along with ten friends and founded an artist-led studio, workshop and gallery space called Loft 6D. A successful art space, it has played host to many artists and musicians, as well as being the place where they founded Ottowin. It's full of many creatives working in different mediums, which makes for a great support network. Without the freedom of the creative space and support from the artist network that it has developed, Ottowin would not have been a possibility. The evolving space and encouraging atmosphere of Loft 6D studios has provided a hotbed of ideas and has pushed both Ollie and Lucy to follow their combined passion.

Their journey to Loft 6D is a gentle cycle ride downhill from where they live in Fishponds, very close to the Bristol to Bath cycle path, which stretches from the city centre near their studio up past their house and on to Bath. A normal day starts early with coffee in their garden at home, then they cycle down the tree-lined, off-road cycle path to their studio for a quick meeting to plan the day ahead (and another coffee). At the moment Ollie spends more time at The Ottowin Shop while Lucy splits her time between the studio and the shop, making orders and creating more stock. They are in the process of building a big workspace in their garden at home, where they will move the Ottowin studio; Loft 6D will be shutting its doors due to rising rental charges – a common problem artists and designers face when working in inner cities.

Ollie and Lucy dream of expanding over the next few years, employing a couple of people who they can pass on their knowledge to and create fulfilling jobs for. They believe making and crafting is good for mental wellbeing; hands-on jobs creates a sense of community and a strong feeling of accomplishment, whilst manipulating materials and making useful artisan objects provides an unparalleled sense of satisfaction.

Ottowin Footwear is sent all over the world through orders placed through the website – they receive orders from Japan to California and everywhere in between. Since opening The Ottowin Shop in the centre of Bristol they have been selling extremely well, while the cherry on the cake for Lucy and Oliver is receiving so much support and appreciation from the city they love and create in.

www.ottowinfootwear.co.uk

Rosalyn Faith

JEWELLERY DESIGNER

Rosalyn's work derives from her passion for constructing textiles using the timeless technique of knit. She transforms her textiles into precious metals, bringing a sculptural element to the material, which is then assembled and embellished with precious and semi-precious stones, creating both intricate, delicate and wearable jewellery.

Rosalyn grew up in a cottage on the outskirts of Cambridgeshire. From a young age she took a practical and visual interest into how things are made, perhaps influenced by her engineering and musician father and lightly artistic mother and sister who inspired her earlier years. Rosalyn originally trained in Textile Design, where she specialised in constructing materials through knitting unconventional yarns, creating sculptural 3D textiles. Through understanding her passion for sculptural materials, she continued her studies, learning new metal-working techniques such as gold- and silversmithing; bringing her two disciplines together, she is now on an exciting journey creating her own collections of contemporary jewellery.

After graduating, she made the move west to begin an internship with metal work artist Rebecca Gouldson. Rebecca specialises in etched metal wall art for galleries, commissioned spaces and homes. Rosalyn worked with Rebecca for six months, learning the inner workings of an independent self-employed artists' studio, and what it takes to be successful. Rebecca had a very structured work ethos which Rosalyn was grateful for; seeing first-hand how passionate and motivated you have to be to make your business a success.

As fate would have it, as soon as Rosalyn completed the internship a studio became available within Centrespace, so she jumped at the opportunity to be part of the studio complex.

Rosalyn feels she would be lost without her creative network in Bristol; she has a close group of jeweller friends who she has learnt a great deal of technical skill from and turn to for advice. There is also a huge range of multi-disciplined artists and designers at Centrespace studios who she is able to talk to about work and get a different perspective. 'Bristol's creative energy and pace has kept me motivated and spurred me to keep creating work. If I'm lacking inspiration there's always something to do or see here. Having a creative hub encourages me to keep progressing and enjoying my work.'

Bristol's creative energy and pace keeps Rosalyn motivated and spurs her on to keep creating work; if lacking in inspiration, there's always something to do or see in the city. Having a creative

hub encourages her to keep progressing and enjoying the work. Finding inspiration in both urban and natural environments, Rosalyn is mostly drawn to interesting surfaces, colours and textures, which Bristol is overwhelmed with. 'I adore the Bristol landscape, I like takings walks around the harbour or going up to Clifton Suspension Bridge and looking down at the textural and dramatic cliff faces. I also like to take trips to the Bristol Museum to look at the ancient Egyptian artifacts; the museum also has a great collection of rocks and minerals which I find beautiful and inspiring.'

Rosalyn has learnt so much from the makers and artists within her studio: Jessica Turrell, Jilly Morris and Dail Behennah in particular have encouraged and informed her practice. Further afield, the life and work of Romilly Saumarez Smith humbles Rosalyn and reminds her of the struggle others face to follow their creative path (Smith is a jeweller who, over the past ten years, has lost the use of her hands through a neurological illness. However, with assistance, she continues to create her beautiful and imaginative items of jewellery). 'I am very lucky to have such creative, powerful and inspiring women in my life!'

Textiles has a profound influence on Rosalyn's work; fabric is more than just the clothes we wear or the curtains we hang – it holds cultures, heritage and identity. She is currently undertaking a couple of commissions using customer's own family heirlooms and re-working them to make bespoke pieces.

Similarly to Milly Melbourne, Rosalyn looks at textiles and jewellery from an anthropological perspective, capturing photographs of the natural and urban landscape through pattern, surface, colour and texture. Her dream project would be to visit communities throughout the world that have been affected by the increase of Western textile manufacturing; many traditional textile techniques are being lost, with employment along the way. Rosalyn would like to work on a project with these communities to help preserve the techniques – with the outcome being in the form of metal jewellery which could last forever.

www.rosalynfaith.com

Rachel Foxwell

CERAMICIST

Rachel makes process-based earthenware vessels using ceramic slabs that act as a canvas; turning a 2D abstract painting into a usable 3D objet d'art. Her work is a culmination of intuitive line, form and colour on minimal forms. The mark making is contemplative, tactile and painterly, reminiscent of a warm breezy day at the beach, and drawing upon coastal landscapes.

Complex layers of slips and engobes are meticulously applied to thin clay slabs. The slabs are later assembled to create simple, geometric forms, marrying form and surface so they become one indivisible unit. The smooth and rough exterior of the vessel is juxtaposed against the glossy slippery interior, much like a shell you would find buried in the sand. Each vessel is slab-built using white earthenware clay. The surface patterns and textures are created using slips containing varying amounts of commercial stains. Rachel fires up her electric kiln to 1,000 degress and then each piece is sanded and glazed with a glossy earthenware glaze. The final stage is a 1,120 degree re-fire, before giving each piece a sand and polish. 'My range of vessels are simple yet contemplative. They stand individually with style and elegance or as a small group, which collectively unite through colour, scale and movement to create a defined space.'

Somerset-born Rachel moved to Bristol ten years ago after studying on the ceramics course at Cardiff University, where Geoffrey Swindell was her tutor. Convinced by her partner to make the move from nearby Bath to Bristol with the promise of a diverse creative city (with a garden studio thrown in) she agreed, and hasn't looked back.

Rachel's studio is in the back garden, built by her husband to suit her 5ft 2in height. It has had many revamps over the years but offers a low-cost studio that makes work/life balance around a young family more attainable. Previously, Rachel was based in a large communal studio cooperative in Bath, and although it was a lot of fun, she admits to enjoying the solitude of her own space.

With her youngest now in full-time education, Rachel has given the shed/studio a makeover and made it as functional as possible so that she can concentrate on her work five days a week. It is also a chance to begin networking within the huge creative community that Bristol houses. Rachel has recently begun selling her work at Flux, a shop that represents many talented designer/makers from Bristol, and later this year she will be taking part in an exhibition about colour and form at Thrown, a contemporary ceramics gallery in London. With time, her ambition is to take part in the big contemporary craft fairs and grow her online presence, adding a shop to the website so that her work becomes more accessible to the public. Basing herself in Bristol

has certainly affected her practice, not in an obvious visual way but certainly day to day; Rachel used to work in a tunnel vision way, believing that to achieve all that she wanted she had to be in the studio constantly making. However, with so much going on around her in Bristol, she has slowly learnt to take time away from the shed in order to explore the rich array of museums, shops, parks and architecture the city has to offer.

Rachel's dream project would be to travel to a location and document the colour changes, textures and patterns of a particular landscape through photography and translate it all into a collection of large vessels for a big white space, with her photographs and vessels being exhibited together.

In her spare time Rachel enjoys heading out in her camper van to explore the landscapes surrounding Bristol; the peaks of the Brecon Beacons and rugged Cornwall coastline are particular favourites and feed back into her work. Rachel is inspired by both rural and urban environments and explores the dichotomy between them; the lines, patterns and colours that feature throughout. The rows of colourful houses in Hotwells that reflect in the water at the harbourside are just as important as the ever-changing colour of a coastal horizon.

Rachel is influenced by minimalist architecture and abstract paintings, there is a clear link between her work and that of colour theory paintings by Josef Albers and Rothko. Like a magpie, she collects image upon image of minimal, colour block architecture, interiors, prints, sculptures and paintings to pin onto her studio walls to reference in the future.

www.rachelfoxwell.co.uk

Ami Pepper

JEWELLERY DESIGNER

Born in Pembrokeshire in west Wales, Ami's unique sculptural pieces of jewellery explore the intricate cluster formations of shells. Her inspiration and love of shells derives from her childhood memories of beachcombing along the Pembrokeshire coast, the cycles of the tides washing ashore organic forms that offer intricate textures, forms and tones. Her work highlights beauty in the smaller, fragile and often forgotten corners of the ocean. 'Growing up on the Pembrokeshire coast has allowed nature to inspire my work consciously and subconsciously. Gathering beach-combed treasures, the textures, cluster formations and tones play a continuous influence in my work.'

Sculpting her jewellery in the shapes and textures of shells that are left behind on the beach like abandoned homes, meticulously hand-carving, casting into metal and encrusted with stones, to form precious yet organic compositions. Ami carves the shells out of wax and then casts them in metal. The jewellery is both visually striking and tactile; you can run your finger over the shells and feel the fine ridges cast in metal, etched by time.

The concept of time plays an important role in her work, as do the cycles of life and nostalgia for home, or *hiraeth* a Welsh word which cannot be translated, it means more than simply 'missing home'. To some, it implies the meaning of missing a time, an era, a place, a person, etc. It is bound with the bittersweet memory of missing something or someone, whilst being grateful for their existence. 'I source organic materials from the landscape and other materials are sourced from all over the world. Sourcing materials in the jewellery trade takes time as it's like being a part of a secret club, you form relationships and there is a big level of trust.'

Ami began her studies on the foundation course at Central Saint Martins in London and went on to graduate with a first class BA(Hons) from the prestigious School of Jewellery in Birmingham in 2013. Since graduating, Ami has become an award-winning jeweller; in 2015 she won the graduate bursary to exhibit at the UK's premier exhibition of fine contemporary jewellery at Goldsmiths' Fair. Julia Peyton-Jones, the Director of the Serpentine Galleries, selected Ami's work as one of the Fairs' highlights; the selected piece then sold to international jewellery collector Tuan Lee.

Ami moved to Bristol after graduating to begin working for Polly Wales, a successful jewellery designer specialising in gemstone pieces and currently based in Los Angeles, USA. Ami now works part-time for Diana Porter, contemporary jeweller, in the centre of Bristol, and has built up a solid network of friends and jewellery designers who she relies on for support and critique.

At the end of 2017 Ami became a member of Centre Space studios. It had been a dream since arriving in Bristol to base herself there; working as a cooperative creates a sense of community, commitment and belief in all the artists based there. To top it off, to reach the studio in the morning she has the pleasure of walking along Bristol Harbour – one of her favourite parts of the day. The work of Adam Buick and Brendan Stuart Burns are on display in Ami's studio; their relationship to the Pembrokeshire coast is translated beautifully in their work and reminds Ami of home. 'I don't think Bristol has influenced my aesthetic, but the city definitely gives me drive and determination.'

Ami has many hopes and dreams for the future; at the top would be to build a studio by the sea (preferably Pembrokeshire) and raise a family in that environment. From a work perspective the dream is to exhibit her work abroad, in New York and LA specifically, and to make her practice full-time and work on collaborations with high-profile clients such as the V&A. 'We live in a time where people are moving so fast and there are so many ways to sell your work. I believe it can take your whole career to figure out where to sell most of your work. Finding the balance and a platform you feel most comfortable with takes time and confidence.'

www.amipepper.com

Eily O'Connell

JEWELLERY DESIGNER

Eily O'Connell conjures up hybrid treasures, illuminating absurd beauty in all natural forms. Using man's destruction of nature as inspiration in a bid to illuminate the harm we are doing to our planet is a basis for her work. This brings about an eerie and macabre feel to the pieces; each piece morphs into a new species through the process of combining natural forms and casting them into metal, adorning them with gemstones, enamel and other curios. Creating wearable macabre treasures that have a mysterious and otherworldly presence, Eily carefully selects an assortment of natural forms that each have appeal and intrinsic character. 'I grew up in a tiny fishing village on the north-west coast of Ireland. I spent all my spare time making things, painting and collecting shells, so it was never a question that I was going to be anything other than some form of artist.'

Eily grew up in Donegal on the north-west coast of Ireland, hence sea themes are evident throughout her work. There are constant references to the human manipulation of nature as Eily is concerned with our ecological impact and so tries to highlight important issues through her pieces and collections. She is influenced by the work of Terhi Tolvanen's and Helen Britton's jewellery; their forms, colours, materials and boldness.

Eily's favourite aspect of creating jewellery is crafting something bespoke in her unique style. With an avid eye for the unusual and textured, she has created some extraordinary pieces, from designing engagement and wedding bands, reviving and re-melting heirlooms to simply casting a small silver pendant from an acorn found in a garden. Her starting point is foraging around beaches, forests and any areas of natural interest to find materials that she can combine and cast into gold and silver to make beautifully detailed jewellery with gemstone and enamel accents. A favourite scouting spot in Bristol is Leigh Woods; a wilderness of tranquility set against Brunel's famous suspension bridge, it offers 2km of woodland on the south-west side of the Avon Gorge.

Eily made the move to Bristol in April 2016, as she had heard so many positive comments about the place. It has a warm and welcoming village mentality but with easy access to London, whilst also having easy access to beautiful countryside and a short drive to the coast. The nurturing and positive attitude of the people won Eily over and now she calls the city home.

Eily lives in the Stokes Croft area of town, which has a bustling creative vibe about it. Outside of the studio, Eily enjoys an array of hobbies including stone faceting, surfing, hillwalking, camping – anything that gets her outdoors. 'I have lots of creative friends I can bounce ideas off. It's always good to have a support network around. This also leads back to a nice studio environment where various disciplines weave together.'

Sourcing only the highest quality materials from her community of suppliers and dealers she has gathered over ten years in business. Using recycled metal where possible and fairtrade stones, Eily also cuts some of the stones herself at Bristol's very own lapidary group; this has been an invaluable asset for Eily as there are not many lapidary groups left in the UK. 'The lapidary class is run by two of the loveliest and most talented old men who are a wealth of knowledge about everything stone-related. One of them, who is my main teacher, Tony Burston, has won first in the world faceting competition, twice. Learning from their pool of knowledge has been marvellous.'

Eily sells most of her work through her own website and at tradeshows, undertaking many commissioned pieces that are often remote through email correspondence. She has also recently opened a pop-up atelier in the centre of Bath that acts as a workshop and showroom; next to Bath Thermae Spa, it is a perfect location to attract those looking to indulge themselves or commission a special piece for an engagement, wedding or birthday. The space is half-workshop and half-showroom, where you can view a wide selection of work. It has offered Eily the perfect chance to meet new customers and gain from invaluable feedback. Her ambition is to have a permanent set-up somewhere, splitting her time between making and selling directly to customers.

www.eilyoconnell.com

Jennifer Orme

CERAMICIST

Jen hand-builds decorative and functional vessels from porcelain, flax and paper clays. She works with printed and stained flat sheets of clay creating forms and smooth matt surfaces that aim to capture the nature of paper.

Working in clay provides an addictively tactile experience, both during the making and as a finished piece. Jen is drawn to the alchemy in the kiln which allows raw clay to develop a purpose. The decoration of the vessels has been distilled from an exploration of the domestic; from the flat chalky panes of colour of the still life paintings of Wayne Thiebaud and Euan Uglow to the descriptive patterns of Henri Matisse's interiors and the wallpaper of Lucienne Day. She is inspired by surfaces; how things look like they feel and how they actually feel. They could be physical objects; the wood worn on the end of a bannister from many hands or a representation of a silk dress in a Reynold's painting. Jen is particularly drawn to the domestic, and the materials and craft disciplines that we have used functionally and decoratively in our homes for centuries; wood, fabric and clay in all their guises. 'I am inspired by simplicity, by how little information is required to suggest a surface like the flat chalky panes of colour in a Euan Uglow painting or the use of pattern to describe a shape in art deco fashion drawing.'

Hailing from Exeter in Devon, Jen spent her childhood in the 1970s and '80s wearing batwing jumpers, curating her bedroom, and endless 'making' projects with friends. While she was a creative child, drawing wasn't her 'thing' and so she dropped art after GCSE and pursued other interests; studying Hispanic Studies at Birmingham University, working for a publishing company, and engaging in random craft projects for a good few years before the urge to 'make' became too great. In her late twenties, Jen made the decision to begin an art foundation course at Cordwainers College in London.

After eight years living and working in London, both Jen and her partner wanted to be closer to family and the countryside. Bristol offered the best of both; it's equidistant from their families in Exeter and Poole and big enough to not feel like they were moving to the back of beyond. Other than the basics, Jen knew very little about the city but as they put down roots she discovered what an amazing place Bristol is: a strong sense of community, liberal, independent, hugely creative and with a healthy dose of anarchy.

Following her move to Bristol Jen began a part-time MA in Multidisciplinary Printmaking at UWE. She enjoyed many aspects of art and design and was excited to see what direction her practice would take, but ultimately wanted to fully engage with one thing and to master it. She found ceramics almost immediately during a workshop on paper clay. Little did she know then that ceramics will not be mastered – it is a forever learning curve.

Jen met a talented and creative group of mums when her daughter was born. They have been her mainstay over the years, emotionally and developmentally, and she regularly meets up with them for a coffee or lunch to share frustrations, achievements and ideas. In 2016, she was chosen for the Crafts Council Hothouse programme, which is a six-month intensive business development course for emerging makers. The alumni number roughly 250, many of whom are based in Bristol, and is a network that Jen relies on both locally and nationally. Fellow maker Angie Parker in particular has given a tremendous amount of encouragement and inspired Jen with her sheer determination and passion.

After several years of renting studio spaces in Bristol, Jen converted her large garage at home to act as a studio and whilst not a beautiful space architecturally, the light is wonderful with large north- and south-facing windows. The benefit of this set-up means that she can pop into the studio at 11 p.m. to wrap a piece of work so that it dries evenly or at 6 a.m. can take the bungs out of the kiln. Jen is lucky to have Ashton Court right on her doorstep; a large estate that was bequeathed to the people of Bristol by the Smyth family, who occupied the estate for 400 years. Within minutes she can be in the countryside, walking by the deer park or up through the woods to a fabulous view of the city, which is a wonderful antidote to working from home when 'studio fever' sets it. 'I open the back door with a cup of tea in one hand and my mobile and sketchbook tucked under my arm. I then open the garage door, go through the cool, dark space of tools and bikes and arrive into the light.'

Jen's current favourite place to explore is Underfall Yard, a historic working boatyard on Spike Island that promotes maritime skills and offers studio spaces to artisans working in this field. It is a wonderful place to people watch against the backdrop of multi-coloured houses of Hotwells and Cliftonwood beyond.

Having recently returned to making following a year living in Sweden with her partner and children, Jen is eager to start making with her hands once again. It takes a while to tune into the clay, to recognise the exact moment when a sheet of clay can be formed into a shape or a pot is dry enough to fettle. She is using this time to explore Scandinavian influences, to test the limits of what is possible and to challenge herself to leave function to one side for the time being.

For now, Jen's work is sold solely through her website whilst she gets back into making and pulling together a collection. This makes sense from an administrative point of view, as her technique is time-consuming and lends itself to very small batch production and one-offs. The challenge lies in finding the time to promote, network and ultimately sell the work. Being a self-employed craftsperson requires a certain level of self-promotion which doesn't come naturally to many people including Jen; putting yourself out there on as many platforms as possible is hard work. A great way to do this is to take part in markets and trade shows where other makers are in the same boat and can offer that understanding and support to one another, something Jen is excited to get back into in the near future.

www.fettleandpatience.weebly.com

Kate Bond

SURFACE DESIGNER

Kate designs digitally-printed fabrics, products and surface print designs. Cutting-edge production techniques transfers her artwork onto high-quality fabric, cushions, lampshades, wallcoverings and more! Kate's work has the ability to be bespoke 'one-offs' or licensed for larger scale reproduction. The Kate Bond brand adheres to an aesthetic of hand-drawn motifs juxtaposed with delicate paper pleats.

Kate takes pleasure in the contrasts of aesthetics, from nature to the pleating of paper. She enjoys making mathematical patterns appear organic, an area she would like to pursue further at some point, possibly as a PhD. 'Carole Waller was a huge influence on me starting an MA. She encouraged me to go for it! Prior to that I was doing evening classes at her studio, which was a real escape for me. It is mostly down to her that I am doing the work that I do today.'

Kate began her post-school education by completing a HND in Design Crafts, with the aim of going to Loughborough University to complete her degree. After a year at York College of Further and Higher Education she hopped onto the the BA Jewellery and Silversmithing course and left with a First Class Degree. However, Kate has worked in all types of materials including ceramics, resins and electroforming. Recently she completed an MA in Fashion and Textiles at Bath Spa University, where she interned at Ciment Pleating, London, to fully understand the highly skilled processes of fabric pleating used in fashion and interiors.

Kate first moved to Bristol in 2003 and began a PGCE in Design Technology (Product Design) at UWE. It was never her plan to become a teacher and she found the whole concept of speaking in public very stressful. Gradually her confidence grew and she secured her first teaching post at Prior Park College in Bath. Kate is still teaching there today part-time and is in charge of a thriving textiles department.

Over the years Kate has exhibited in many galleries and exhibitions including SOFA Chicago and Lesley Craze Gallery, London. She has also completed a variety of commissions for interior brands, print studios and commercial projects; most recently for Nina Campbell and Willis Newson. Bath Spa University kick-started her creative career. It was a springboard into meeting the right people and securing opportunities that would never have happened otherwise. Due to Nina Campbell being a patron of the university, Kate was asked to create two designs for her; one of the commissions was included in her Coromandel Collection in 2016. 'I am a member of a contemporary textiles group "Seam Collective", which is based in Bath. We are emerging and established embroiderers, printers, knitters, weavers, dyers, fashion designers, eco-designers, makers, artists … As a group we support each other creatively, meet socially and periodically organise group exhibitions.'

Kate is currently working on two large commissions. One is for the new Y Bwthyn Macmillan Specialist Care Unit at the Royal Glamorgan Hospital. It is a 45m square feature wall based on the sweeping landscape of Wales. The mural runs along the main corridor and over windows. The other commission is for St Peter's Hospice in Bristol. This comprises of several murals that depict the landscape and complement the beautiful new interior.

www.katebond.co.uk

Sarah Wilton

CERAMICIST

Sarah is a Fine Art graduate specialising in wheel-thrown ceramic wares with expressive graphic patterns and gestures within the glaze. Completing a Fine Art degree in Sculpture and Print at UWE in Bristol, Sarah was inspired by the sculptural forms of Lucie Rie and the painterly quality and patterns of ceramic designer Jessie Tait, whose whimsical and optimistic designs for Midwinter Pottery are an ongoing source of delight.

In her third year she became completely obsessed with Formica laminate and endeavoured to make sculpture from it. However, she didn't find it very versatile and after receiving the UWE fellowship residency at Spike Island after graduating, Sarah moved into ceramics, which she decided was the perfect material to imprint the patterns she had been making. Sarah follows a strong set of rules for making; each form must be unique with an exploration of colour and have an imprint that is fleeting in someway, showing movement. 'My dad told me to go make some pots. He bought me my pottery wheel, it's an old industrial wheel, a little slow sometimes, but it does the job. I've never made so many and feel like the best is yet to come.'

Her inspiration is eclectic and evolving, a process that combines many sources, such as mid-century British ceramic forms alongside Art Nouveau colours and mediterranean clay bodies. Sarah's love of colour stems from her childhood, when she would open the pots of paint that her painter-decorator father would keep in his yard; the colour cards became her currency with which she could create many combinations. Opening fresh tins of paint and not knowing exactly what colour might be inside gave her a lot of joy, a similar sort of joy that she now gets opening the kiln door; the beauty of ceramics is the alchemy, no one glaze looks the same on a different clay body, fired at varying temperatures – experimentation is boundless.

After completing a Foundation Course in Art and Design, Sarah went to Rio De Janeiro for a fews months in search of bright colours and interesting music. Upon returning she moved to Bristol, where these curiosities continue in the endless streets of colourful houses and the vibrant underground music scene in the city. Shows at the Arnolfini have always been a

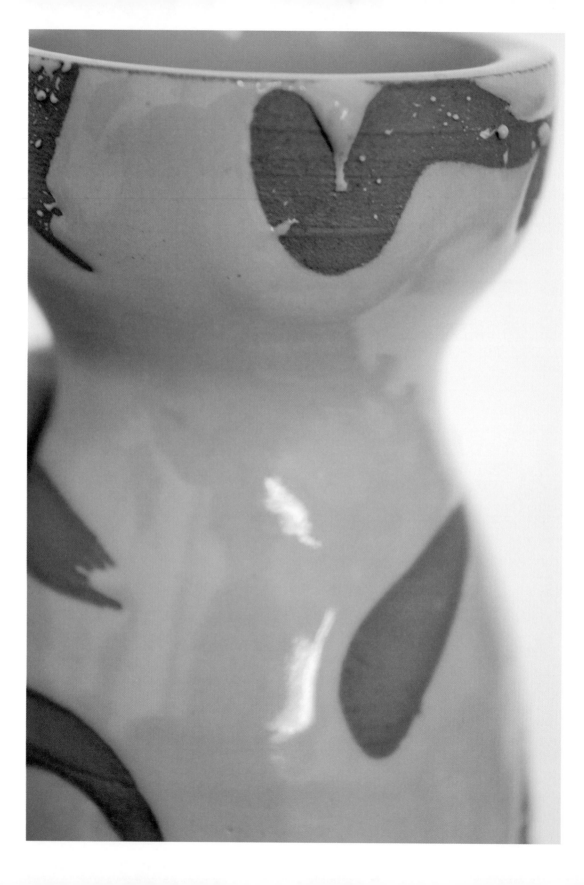

good source of inspiration, the pottery collection at Bristol Museum as well as Bower Ashton UWE library and the beautiful seasonal colours from all the plants of Piet Oudolf's garden at Hauser & Wirth in Bruton, Somerset.

Sarah's studio is at Spike Island; a contemporary art gallery and studio complex near the Bristol harbourside. This seems the perfect place for her to work as they merge fine art and design disciplines within their studios and and have an exciting and engaging programme of exhibitions; recent highlights for Sarah were Alex Concchetti and David Batchelor's Flatlands exhibition, which had a vibrant use of colour.

Sarah is also part of the Network for Creative Enterprise, which is in partnership with pervasive media based at the Watershed, UWE and Spike Island. This network has been very supportive with regard to developing commercial confidence and amplifying opportunities. Of her contemporaries, Sarah finds the artwork of Richard Woods hugely inspiring; his work is multilingual and speaks to both a commercial and contemporary art audience on a large scale. She dreams of developing this within her own practice; the functional ware by Brickett Davda's ceramics, purely for the simple design, muted colour palette and copious amount of tea you can fit into their mugs. Sophie Alda's Klein blue vases and efficiency in her production is something Sarah aspires to; she would love

to spend an extra hour in the studio experimenting, playing around with new shapes, but time is precious and so there is a fine balancing act most days. 'Often, I find people want pieces to be functional and have a purpose, particularly when the objects are of a small scale.'

For Sarah, colours are transitory and any artist experimenting with it interests her: the work by painters such as Joseph Albers, the Expressionists and Cy Twombly and Joan Miró, whose expressive mark making she aspires to. Ettore Sottsass' Totem ceramic sculptures are a recurring revelation; Sarah ponders how to strike a balance between functionality and pure sculpture and admires his unashamed lean towards the later.

She recently completed her first big commission for Liberty London and enjoys taking one-of-a-kind pieces to the DIY art market in Peckham and to the ceramic fair at the Hepworth, Wakefield. In the future she would like to scale up and make batch editions for stockists in the UK and abroad.

Scale is the long-term focus and Sarah is constantly practicing her throwing technique with bigger pieces of clay with a view to make her pieces as a sculptural series. In theory she could commission these larger pieces to be made by someone else for her to decorate, but Sarah is tenacious and wants to have that connection with the work at every stage of the process.

www.sarahwilton.com

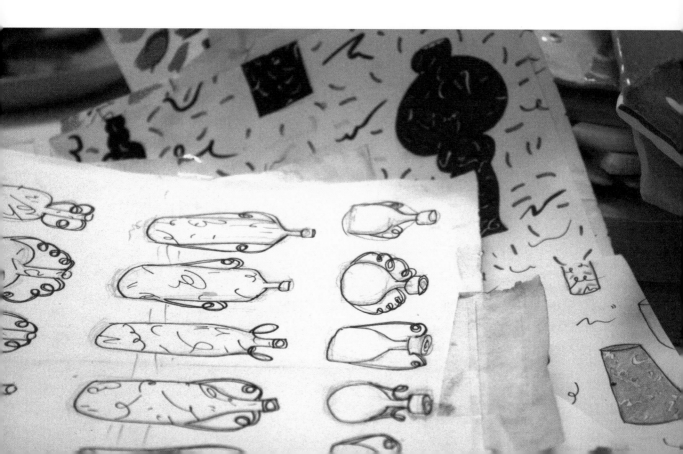

Jessica Thorn

CERAMICIST

The aesthetic and design of manufactured metal tins hasn't changed for over 200 years. Fascinated by this curious fact, Jessica began to design and make ceramic pieces inspired by the characteristics and forms of metal tins through vitrified porcelain. A passion for cooking and eating has naturally influenced Jessica's functional response within her designs.

Many of our conversations have revolved around food and how ceramics play a part in that process; how an everyday ritual can become more pleasurable through the use of a handmade item. With this in mind, she designs and makes functional objects for others and herself by focusing on a simple aesthetic whilst showing off the pure quality of the ceramic. A cup of tea at her studio is served up in one of her own mugs, there is no preciousness to her work – they are to be used and enjoyed every day. 'I love walking around the docks, getting inspiration in Underfall Yard, looking at all of the industrial machines, buildings and surroundings. Also the rust helps to inspire my colour pallette!'

Jessica undertook a Foundation Degree in Art and Design at Plymouth College of Art, where she found the 3D department and cementing her passion for ceramics. The delicate nature of porcelain excited Jess and seemed the obvious material choice to marry contemporary design with her response to old kitchenware. The experimentation of hand building, colouring and polishing porcelain allowed her to express and create an honest contemporary response to her obsession with mass-produced enamelware.

The refined colour pallet was developed from a study into Jessica's fascination with rusting and patination on the surface of metal. The colours derive from the use of coloured slip and non-ceramic materials as leather, copper and cork, providing character, depth and a unique feel for each piece.

Creating valued one-off pieces is essential for Jessica to celebrate making by hand and the handmade culture in Britain. She celebrates craftsmanship through her own work by highlighting her elusive joining technique, allowing the viewer to see the construction and unique trademark of her craft.

After graduating, Jessica moved back to her hometown of Bristol and proceeded to gain exposure and prizes for her work. Bovey Tracey Contemporary Craft Festival crowned her 'Best New Business' and she was selected for Crafts Council Hothouse 5; a business development programme aimed at helping emerging makers. Whilst giving Jessica support in marketing and finance, it also offered an invaluable support network of like-minded designer/makers and most of all it gave her the confidence to go big with her work, to take it to the next level

and believe in herself. Elaine Bolt was assigned as her buddy during Hothouse; watching Elaine's practice blossom has allowed Jessica to feel excited about where her own work can go.

Jessica also took on the position of artist in residence at Mayfield School for Girls, which was a fantastic opportunity and allowed her the time and space needed to focus entirely on her craft; spending time working with clay, developing her own work and knowledge of the materials was a huge privilege. Jessica also enjoyed teaching, which broadened her skillset and gave her a great foundation to build upon when returning to Bristol and setting up her own workspace and ceramic classes.

After completing the artist residency, a spot became available on the ground floor of Centrespace Studios; a well-established co-operative of over thirty professional artists. The studio is vast and gives Jessica space to grow into; she has plans to develop the space to suit her own practice and that of the regular workshops she runs. At lunchtime she pops upstairs to chat with fellow studio holders or grabs lunch at nearby St Nick's Market – a haven for foodies.

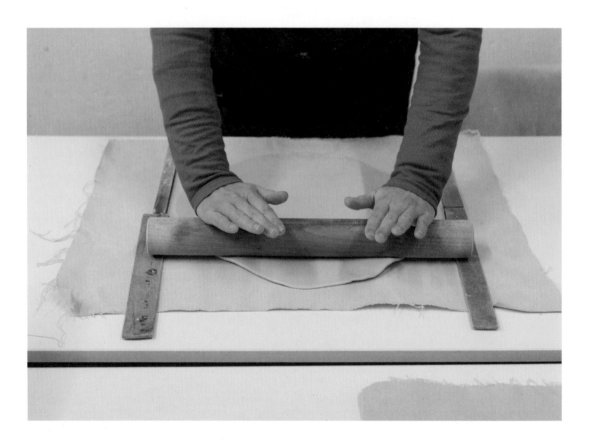

The studio can be pretty chilly so there is normally a cup of tea on the go in a sample Jessicca Thorn cup, Radio 4 on in the background or sometimes a podcast; Jessica's current favourites being 'The Guilty Feminist', 'Made of Human' and Adam Buxton. Once the day is planned out, Jessica can begin the process of wedging, rolling and cutting out the clay for each individual piece. Whilst waiting for it to dry she will finish off any pieces started previously, or will start on a list of jobs such as mixing glazes or slips, designing new pieces or loading kilns. Jessica then joins the pieces freshly rolled that day, making as many as possible. 'I wanted to be part of a community of artists, with a social element to my daily work, as being a maker can be isolating.'

'I would like to continue developing new pieces, maybe scale up slightly. I would like to work on some collaborations with other makers. I would also like to grow my pottery classes, helping to share the sheer joy of making with your hands.' There is much to keep Jessica motivated, not least her friends, family and studio buddies, but also the quiet satisfaction that lies within making; moments of pure bliss in the studio, when a successful kiln firing happens or when a new design pops into her head. Reflecting on how all of the hard work has paid off so far, and the exciting opportunities that lie ahead. At the time of this interview, Jessica is preparing new work for Art in Clay at Hatfield House. She is continuously developing new pieces and enjoying the small pleasures of using ceramics when cooking and eating.

www.jessicathorn.co.uk

Juliet Bailey and Franki Brewer

TEXTILE DESIGNERS

To create a space where avant-garde, innovative fabric design meets traditional manufacturing process has been five years in the making for textile design duo Juliet Bailey and Franki Brewer. They met back in 2008 whilst both working in London – having completed separate degrees in textiles from Brighton and Winchester Universities – and by 2009 had launched their woven textile design studio Dash & Miller together. In 2007 they made the move to Bristol as it suited both their personal and professional lives and in the spring of 2015 The Bristol Weaving Mill opened its roller-shutters for business. 'There is always something new to create; we work as a team in the studio and I love to see everyone's combined skill and creativity coming together to make new and exciting outcomes every day.'

Juliet and Franki had a vision that there would one day be a facility in the UK where a no-boundaries approach could be taken to fabric sampling and production weaving. After years of research this dream became a reality and now the Bristol Weaving Mill contributes to the UK's historical lineage and tradition of weaving and manufacturing.

The Bristol Weaving Mill is a micro-mill based in the heart of Bristol with facilities for creating exclusive, bespoke and experimental fabrics for the international fashion and interior industries. With strong links with the world's most interesting and innovative yarn suppliers, finishers and manufacturers, the Bristol Weaving Mill is an artisanal weaving mill in the unique position to be able to supply an unparalleled level of creativity and innovation for both small and large-scale production runs.

Both Franki and Juliet live outside of Bristol in the Somerset countryside and enjoy the contrast this offers. Their studio is near the Temple Quay development in Old Market in the centre of Bristol. Tucked away behind Brunel's famous railway station in the heart of Bristol, the unmistakable heartbeat of salvaged textile machinery reverberates from within an old red-brick building. This is their third studio location; the first was a live/work space in Banwell, north Somerset, the second was in St Philips through the organisation Bristol Spaceworks, and this third studio is a privately rented space that they share with Bristol Textile Quarter and other companies. The space has been really flexible for their growing business and has allowed them to expand and accommodate

industrial weaving machinery alongside their handlooms. Bristol has allowed them to grow a little faster than perhaps they would have in London, due to the space and network they have access to. They also work with fibre producers from the local areas including Fernhill Farm, who supply some of their locally sourced 100 per cent natural undyed wool.

Working in Bristol offers many perks, not least the international airport which makes visiting clients in Europe and USA fairly straightforward, while the trains and road network mean that their clients in London and suppliers in places like Yorkshire are easy to reach. Most of their work is commissioned through one-on-one (or one-on-two) meetings and so they travel extensively.

Their signature collection is predominantly focused on wool and fancy tweeds, however, their creative and design-led team have a background in hand-weaving for production that allows for a greater level of responsiveness when developing designs and fabric qualities.

They also focus on creating ecological, sustainable and ethically responsible fabrics using locally spun wool together with recycled and reclaimed fibres wherever possible, with the rare opportunity to focus on accountability, traceability and sustainability from the ground up. They source from all over the UK as well as from smallholders and farmers in Italy, Japan, Germany and Peru. A dream commission would be to work closely with Burberry to develop sustainable fabrics for their collection.

Juliet and Franki are currently developing some beautiful hand-woven linen-blend fabrics for private clients, ranging from Austrian and Italian couturiers to British interior designers. They are also developing beautiful wool and wool-blend scarves and throws for clients all over the UK, alongside catwalk fashion fabric for clients in the USA. 'It would be amazing to curate an exhibition for our ten-year anniversary that celebrates modern craft in design.' Their most exciting upcoming project is working with Babs Behan from Botanical Inks on the 'Bristol

Cloth', a run of fabric and product working in a closed-loop system with fibre from Fernhill Farm just outside of Bristol. After nine years in the industry they have a lot of respect for other females working hard to create beautiful and ethically produced textiles such as Botanical Inks, Tamay & Me and Antiform; all Bristol-based designers. 'Remember to celebrate the successes. It's so easy to focus on the challenges and the pitfalls that they can often eclipse the triumphs and achievements that we all constantly work hard for.'

Their passion and drive to continue growing and developing what they have created is inspiring, as is their love of woven fabrics and the joy of working with a customer to design and develop a beautiful fabric for them from fibre to finished product. From an heirloom product for an individual to a bulk order of fashion fabric for an international designer, there are endless possibilities and ideas that come with working in a small close-knit team.

www.bristolweavingmill.co.uk

Phoebe Smith

CERAMICIST

Phoebe is a ceramic artist living and working in Bristol from her home studio where she runs her own practice alongside teaching. Her craft journey began whilst studying for a degree in Embroidery at Manchester Metropolitan University, where she graduated in 2010.

Phoebe's work is inspired by memories of land, sea and sky. Her connection to the natural environment is visceral and is an integral part of her artistic expression. She is less motivated by a desire to express a literal representation of her experience, but rather a sense of the feelings and moods imparted on her by her journeys through the English countryside. Her current body of work draws specifically on memories of summers from her childhood home in north Norfolk, of dusty sunsets, rolling fields and big horizons. It is her hope that the ethereal quality of mark making and chosen tones with the fluid forms she creates make for more than just a visual experience but take on a much more physical presence. 'I grew up in the countryside in Norfolk which I think attributes to my connection with the land and sea. Memories of dusty horizons and coastal walks very much inform the aesthetics of my work past and present.'

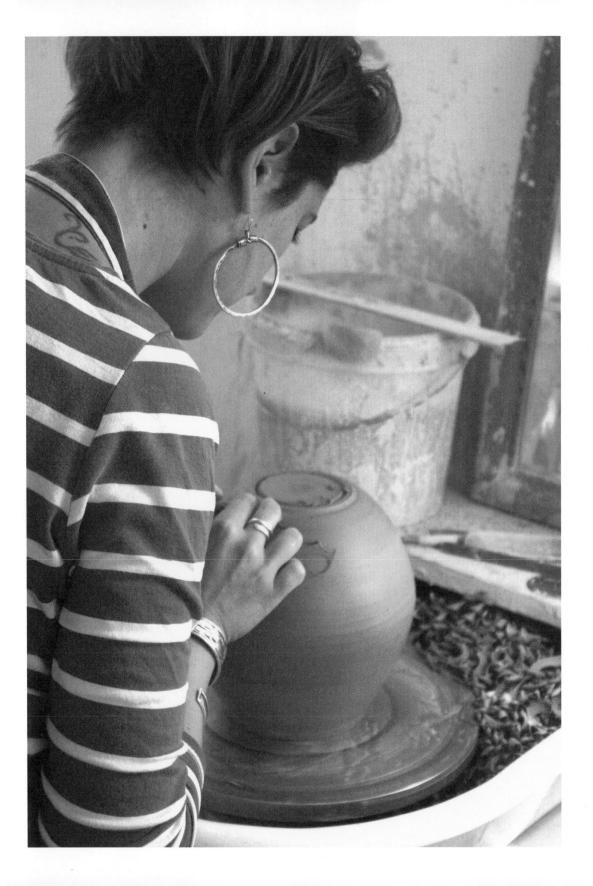

It was during her initial studies that she developed a fascination in the process of turning raw materials into new objects of function and beauty.It is imperative to her that a true understanding of the boundaries in which the craft and process exists is maintained at all times. The way in which the creative process meets the utilitarian in functional ceramics drives her work, blurring the boundaries of the precious with the everyday object, creating elegant forms that are perfect for their intended use in the home.

After university Phoebe's increasing interest in three-dimensional forms drew her to explore ceramics, where in pottery classes she felt an instant affiliation with both material and process. Despite working in a very different medium with completely different processes from that of her early studies, Phoebe still draws on the lessons in creative practice and exploration of ideas learnt during her degree.

Her move to Bristol followed a very conscious decision to move forward with her creative career, to really focus on learning and understanding the details of her chosen craft, ceramics.

Upon moving to Bristol Phoebe rented a space at Maze Studios, where she dedicated her time in learning firstly how to throw and then on building her knowledge of ceramic practice. Phoebe has built a detailed knowledge of her craft, from the preparation of clay, production of work, development of glazes right through to the firing process.

With Bristol being fairly small its very easy to walk about and explore. The environment always influences her creative practice, and she is often making mental notes of colours and textures to bring into her work. Bristol is a wonderfully creative city which is a great push as a maker but also means there is a huge support network of people making similar journeys.

Phoebe is now fortunate to have a studio at the end of her garden, which she converted in 2017. Prior to this she was working full-time whilst trying to set up a business – not the easiest thing to do! Luckily a few things fell into place, enabling her to build a studio, quit her job and begin teaching; creating a structure that enabled her to make proper space for her own practice. 'I teach alongside working on my own practice, which felt like a logical way

to support myself financially but has turned into a really important part of my business, I love passing knowledge on to others, enabling them to flourish in something they love doing.'

Phoebe is currently trying to draw together all that she has learnt over the past ten years to create a product range that she feels best reflects her love of ceramics; pulling together all the ideas, inspiration and explorations into work that succinctly expresses who she is as a maker.

Babs Behan

BOTANICAL ARTIST

Botanical Inks is a natural dye studio based in Bristol, founded by botanical artist Babs Behan. It offers small-scale natural dyeing services for designers and businesses, and a platform for re-skilling creative communities with local plant knowledge and contemporary traditional 'low-impact' surface application techniques.

Babs also teaches people to forage for local colour-producing plants and how to use a variety of dye and print processes, without the use of any toxic synthetic chemicals or heavy metals, prioritising the use of local, organic, ethically sourced and manufactured materials, such as dyes from local organic farm and food waste, locally grown and manufactured wool, organic British peace silk, recycled British paper and vintage or second-hand garments and textiles. 'Promoting earth-friendly and biologically nutritious products is integral to our mission.'

By using regenerative, biological materials, which are safe to use and put back into the earth after their use, Botanical Inks offer an alternative to the toxic petrochemical, and highly processed, art and design mediums and practices which have otherwise become the norm.

Babs' journey to this specialist area of textile production was not a straightforward one; a free spirit, she didn't take to mainstream education and preferred to skip school so that she could be free to do whatever she chose. However, she always did well in art and dreamed of pursuing life at art college in London, and so she did a foundation course at University College London (UCL) only to feel disillusioned by the course, the people and city life. Babs soon realised a BA in Fine Art wasn't for her and switched to Surface Pattern, where she believed a career could be carved out more easily.

A friend was travelling in India and wrote to her about a block print house she had visited, where they used vegetable inks to print silk, cotton and cotton paper with wooden hand-carved blocks. Finally, she arranged a trip to go and study with the master dyer and his family in Jaipur. She learned each step of the process, using her own designs to carve blocks and print cloth.

After university, Babs continued to pursue her passion for exploring the world, using travel as an opportunity to discover more about indigenous textiles and natural dye traditions. Babs immersed herself in the festival lifestyle; she recycled end of roll block printed silk and cotton from the family she had studied with in Jaipur to make playsuits to wear and sell at festivals, spending her summers in England at festivals and winters in India to produce her new collections. After six years, the travelling artisan lifestyle had become exhausting and she needed to find another way to structure her life.

After an incredible heart-aligning journey through Costa Rica and California, Babs returned to the UK to start a new chapter. She didn't want to be in London anymore and felt a strong draw to Bristol; she knew some good people in the city and felt inspired by the projects she knew about. Bristol seemed like the Emerald City; it had a reputation for being alternative and environmentally conscious.

Babs gets much of her inspiration from Rebecca Burgess, who pioneered Fibershed in California; Rebecca originally started out by trying to wear only clothes which had been grown and made within 150 miles of where she lived in Northern California. It was almost impossible to begin with and instead she had to make them herself with local fibre, but it would have taken years to make an entire wardrobe from scratch. So she mapped out all of the growers, farmers, spinners, weavers, knitters, tailors, etc. in the region and connected them together to

start making the process easier. She eventually managed to make her 150-mile wardrobe by connecting the dots and collaborating with the various artisans to make naturally dyed local fibre garments. These consisted mainly of knitted, hand-woven and felted garments. What became apparent was that a locally produced cloth was missing entirely from the chain.

Babs recently launched her first book *Botanical Inks: Plant-to-Print Dyes, Techniques and Projects* with Quadrille Books. This step-by-step guide is for anyone wanting to work with natural dyes. It takes you through all the basics, from how to extract dyes from different plant materials and how to transform these into plant-based printing inks, paints, writing inks,to using different techniques, like bundle dyeing with fresh flowers, organic indigo dyeing, shibori tie dye, block print and screen print with natural dyes.

She is also soon to launch the Bristol Cloth Project. This was initially launched in 2015 with the Bristol Weaving Mill; they sourced the weave design through a nationwide competition and awarded the winner with the first 6m of the woven cloth. The cloth is made with Romney-Shetland lambswool from Fernhill Farm in the Mendips and biologically washed and spun before going to Botanical Inks in Old Market to be hand-dyed with organic local plant dyes – madder, a red root, and weld, a yellow flowering plant – to make an orange, which sits next to the two undyed natural fleece colours in brown and beige. Once dyed, the yarn is then taken to the Bristol Weaving Mill to be woven on their loom.

Through crowdfunding, they are on target to raise £20,000 to produce the first 200m of the finished cloth; it's a woollen tweed cloth and they will be pre-selling it by the metre through the crowdfunder campaign for local designers to buy and make bioregional garments, interior items and accessories. 'In the UK we have lost our local textile economy, shipping it out to Asia for the past hundred years and more, where it is cheaper and reliant often on slave labour and toxic chemical processes. It is my dream to be able to use a non-toxic British-grown-and-made cloth to make garments in the UK, and the Bristol Cloth is my starting point.'

Babs runs many workshops across the UK and hopes to set up her own workshop space in Bristol soon.

www.botanicalinks.com

About the Author

Sophie Rees grew up near Abergavenny in South Wales and studied Fine Art Painting in both Bath and Brighton before moving to East London. In 2009 she co-founded a studio and exhibition complex in Hackney Wick, a regeneration area of East London opposite the 2012 Olympic stadium. It is here she began curating exhibitions and project managing events such as a monthly design market for designer/makers living in the local area. From this she founded the agency Designers/Makers which has grown to become a national membership organisation; providing events, PR, business advice, an online shop and opportunities for its members. The agency works in partnership with other creative organisations including the Design Museum, Southbank Centre, Arnolfini, the V&A and the Old Truman Brewery, London.

www.designersmakers.com

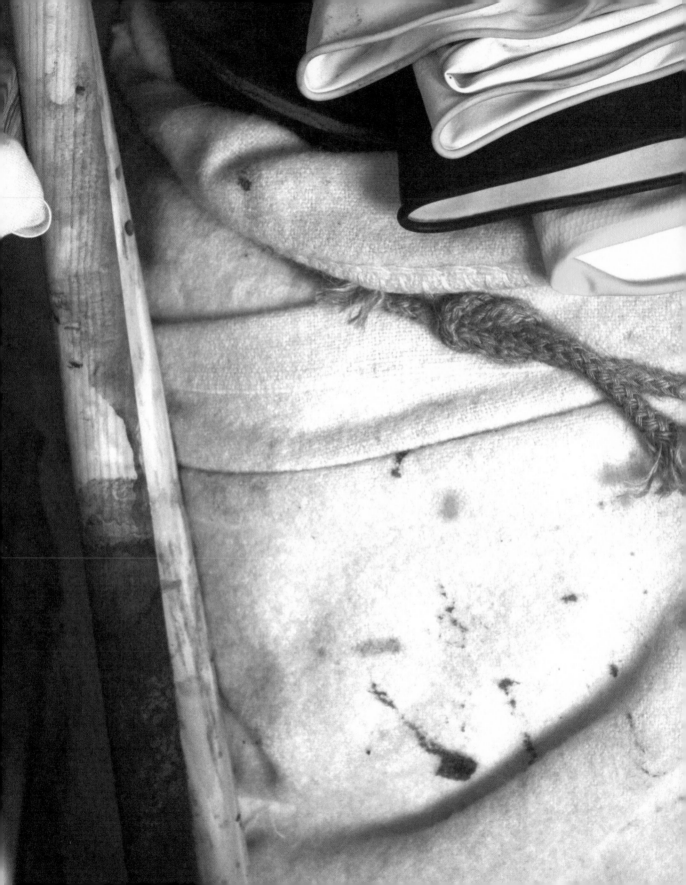

Acknowledgements

Thank you to my family for their ongoing support and belief in my endeavours.

This book would not have been possible without the enthusiasm and commitment from all the designers; thank you for inviting me into your workspace.

Image Credits

All photography within the book was taken by Sophie Rees, excluding the following:

Katie Wallis
Pages 18 & 20 © Jo Hounsome Photography

Milly Melbourne
Pages 24 & 27 © Milly Melbourne

Sophie Woodrow
Pages 31, 32 & 34 © Sophie Woodrow

Stephanie Tudor
Pages 38, 42 & 43 © Stephanie Tudor
Page 41 © Yesenia Thibault Picazo

Angie Parker
Pages 46 & 48 (*bottom*) © Yeshen Venema

Libby Ballard
Pages 52 & 55 © Emma Harrel

Liz Vidal
Page 60 © Liz Vidal

Anna Gravelle
Page 70 © Stephen Lethal
Pages 65 & 66 © Yeshen Venema

References

http://museums.bristol.gov.uk/narratives.php?irn=8798
www.bristol-glass.co.uk/history.html
www.britannica.com/art/Bristol-ware